How to
Remember Bible Verses

Paul Mellor

Copyright © 2018 by Paul Mellor

ISBN 978-0692187142

In Memory of Tamra Joy

TABLE OF CONTENTS

INTRODUCTION

It's a sun-drenched mid-summer morning as I make my way on Storrow Drive. The city is already bustling. I see walkers, runners, and cyclists maneuvering by the esplanade. I see sailors and rowers out on the glistening waters of the Charles River, and over at Fenway Park, ballplayers are getting ready to take to the field. Yes, Boston is on the move.

Growing up in nearby Rhode Island, I had visited the hub too many times to count. I've explored almost the entire city. I've walked the Freedom Trail, run the Boston Marathon, ridden on all the subway lines, and roamed the hallways under the gold dome on Beacon Hill.

Kenmore Square to Haymarket Square, Custom House to the State House, Public Garden to Boston Garden, North End to South Station, I've seen it all. However, on this July day in 2018, I was going to a place I had never been.

Exiting off of Storrow Drive I turn right to begin my drive across the Longfellow Bridge when I see my destination; Massachusetts Institute of Technology (MIT). I arrive on time.

My path to MIT began in 1992 when, at age 34 and a member of the Richmond Toastmasters Club, I was in search of a speech topic. I was doing a lot of that ever since I had joined Toastmasters. I had given talks on a wide-range of topics. My file cabinet drawer is full of speeches, but little did I know that on the afternoon of December 31, at the Bon Air Library in Richmond, I found *The Memory Book* by Harry Lorayne and Jerry Lucas. A few weeks later I gave a 6-minute talk, without notes, and subsequently developed such a passion for the topic, that giving talks on memory skills is a full-time job, or better yet, a full-time calling.

I've been blessed that companies and associations have compensated me to travel to their headquarters and conferences enabling me to share that passion with so many people in all 50 states. Through my presentations, I show that memory is an acquired skill. My intent is to show how memory can be improved. So far, so good, but that success has come from a little help from above.

Our God-given brains are more powerful than any computer or gadget we could ever own. Instantly, we're able to conjure up images and pictures at will. Our brains are downright smart. And it was my brain that got me to MIT.

For me to get to MIT, I first had to get to an MRI. I was contacted by Princeton University researcher Ken Norman. I would come to Princeton for a two-day study on my brain. Researchers would monitor my thought process as I lie still for hours.

I was given several numbers to memorize as Ken and his team looked at my brain activity while taking over 8000 photos of what goes on between my ears. In two months they would report their findings during the finals of the USA Memory Championship at MIT.

As I sat on stage at the Kresge Auditorium listening to the findings from Chris Baldassano, I thanked God that there certainly was something between my ears.

On a big screen in front of a large audience that included reporters from CBS News, Chris lays out interesting discoveries. He highlights the areas of my brain that is bright red. He states that most people have this brightness in their brains when they are actually *seeing* something. What's interesting, Chris notes, is that Paul wasn't seeing anything. His eyes were closed and he was only imagining. Paul was able to recall all the numbers by his skill of linking pictures to mental anchors, he says.

As I walked off stage, I remained steadfast that everyone can improve their memory. Applying our God-given abilities to imagine, to visualize, to link new information to what we already know may not get you to an MIT stage, but it will help you in every aspect of your life, including techniques for remembering Bible verses.

No pills needed. The answers to our memory deficiencies are already in our heads. God only knows.

IN THE BEGINNING

I t's the #1 best-selling book of all time. Most likely, you have it on your bookshelf. In fact, you may own more than one copy. But before you seek divine intervention or pray about what it is, let me tell you; it's the Bible.

Everyday millions of people reach out to the Bible seeking comfort, wisdom, and doctrine from its pages. However, sometimes it's difficult to remember what we read and to locate a verse we want to review.

Therefore, THIS book will help in remembering THAT book. The key word is 'remembering.' It is not design to interpret. The **ONLY** objective of this book is to show you how to ...

REMEMBER

You won't hear your Preacher from Providence or your Minister from Minnesota explain the Bible like the way it's explained here. However, reading and understanding this book will help you remember what they say. The method is unconventional and at times, may seem odd, but it works.

The systems are built around an organized and efficient pattern. It's based on how our minds work when we want to recall new information.

People learn by doing and we're going to be utilizing that principle in remembering verses. We're going to be using our imaginations in a way we never thought possible. As children we did this very well. We pretended we were cowboys or Indians; doctors or lawyers; baseball players or ballerinas. Put us in a room for hours and we would have sailed across the seas, blasted off to space, and climbed the highest peaks, all before going to bed. But as we grew older it's our imaginations that have gone to bed. As adults, visualizing and pretending is seldom done.

We put ourselves through school by listening to teachers and reading chapters. We've been told that there are no shortcuts. If we don't understand something we read it again and again and remember just so we can pass the next test. No need to memorize because there'll be new information to learn tomorrow.

Memorizing, we've been told, is a cop out. I can still remember my teacher saying, "I don't want you to memorize it. I want you to know it." Is there a difference? One teacher told me how to remember the Great Lakes by thinking of *HOMES*. Was that cheating? Should I had studied night and day trying to remember the names of Huron, Ontario, Michigan, Erie, and Superior, instead of being taught the *HOMES* technique which took two minutes to learn? I can confidently rattle off the lakes because I memorized a system. Was that bad? I don't think so.

My music teacher taught me how to remember the scales by saying **E**very **G**ood **B**oy **D**oes **F**ine. My father taught me that *Left Loosens* when handing me a screwdriver. The television news anchorman taught me to think *Spring Back* and *Fall Forward* on the eve of changing clocks. I've learned there's nothing wrong with memory shortcuts.

In a highly publicized murder trial a witness tells the jury that he's certain he saw the body after 10:30 pm. How did he remember? He walked his dog after watching the *Mary Tyler Moore* show on television. He used what he already knew to his advantage. It wasn't even asked if he were wearing a watch.

There is so much we already know by using events or moments we've lived through. We remember lyrics to songs that were played years before and recall where we were when the Twin Towers came down on that dark September day.

We can still picture the kitchen in the house where we were raised. We can visualize the schoolyard when we were in Kindergarten. We can remember the taste of our aunt's cherry cheesecake, and recall the smell of grass after mowing our grandparent's lawn.

Our minds are remarkable, but often we don't use what we already know to our advantage. Whether it's learning new math, studying a new language, or trying to remember scripture we do what we've always done. We read and read again, hoping that it eventually sticks.

This book uses information you already know. It opens up an endless supply of possibilities for you to remember and retain to comprehend scripture. I doubt you've ever seen information as the way it's presented here. This book is built on shortcuts. It's constructed in a way that will open your mind to look at scripture in a way you've never seen. Once you learn the memory principles, you'll learn scripture at a quicker pace.

The book is divided into learning three parts; Books of the Bible, Chapters and Verses, and Scripture.

The section on Books of the Bible will show how translating the 66 books into pictures will aid us in remembering. This section is unconventional, but it does work and it's fun.

The section on Chapters and Verses is the most difficult out of the three to learn. You'll need to read the pages of this section slowly so you can fully understand how the system works. But once you grasp it, you're in for an awakening because never again will you search your mind as to what chapter and verse a specific scripture is located. You'll know it.

The third section shows how to break down scripture to find patterns. You'll be able to find memorable patterns to every scripture. 25 examples are given.

Keep this book by your Bible and begin to ***remember***.

The computer is our brain and the components of that brain are the uses of **V**isuals, **I**mages, **N**eighborhoods, and **E**xaggerations. It's the *VINE* system and it's going to help us in remembering the Bible.

Visuals - apple, basketball, watch, yo-yo, french fries, dollar, bike.
Non-visuals - before, of, their, limitation, until, now, quiet.

If you were to draw a picture of each item, which row would you chose? The visuals or the non-visuals? If you chose visuals, you're not alone. Visuals are easier to remember because they're things we can see and touch and taste. Visuals are memorable.

Malachi, Zephaniah, Deuteronomy, Ezekiel and Ecclesiastes are non-visuals. They are hard to remember. It's very difficult to remember these books of the Bible because they are foreign to us. They're hard to picture in our 'mind's eye'. If the books were Malt Shake, Zipper, and Lawn Mower, they'd be easier to recall because we're already familiar with these objects and they're visual.

Use your **Imagination**. If you've purchased a lottery ticket, planted a flower, carried an umbrella, or attended a reunion, then you have an imagination. If you've gone grocery shopping, checked your mailbox, been summoned by your supervisor, or anxiously awaited for your child to come home, then you have an imagination. Imagination is a formation of a mental picture.

If we don't imagine a beautiful flower, then we're not going to bury seeds. If we don't image the chocolate cake, then we're not going to buy the flour. If we don't imagine our hair getting soaked, then we're not going to reach for the umbrella.

There's a lot of imagery in the Bible. When we read about Jonah and the whale, Daniel and the lion, and Eve and the serpent we are using our imaginations. Stories help us see those events. Can you imagine what it must have been like for Jonah to have been swallowed by a fish? Can you imagine how Daniel must have felt when he was thrown into the lion's den? Can you picture Eve eating the apple? Those stories can be visualized and they can be imagined. Those stories are memorable.

Chapters and verses are more difficult to imagine. Chapter 12, verse 5; Chapter 31, verse 15 and Chapter 67, verse 23 create no image. The stories within these chapters might be memorable, but the numbers aren't. We're going to change that.

Neighborhoods are memorable. We close our eyes, yet still recall the neighborhood in which we live. When we think of a house in our own neighborhood we can easily remember the house next door and the house next door to that. One thought leads us to the other. The neighborhood is what we know and we are reminded by the landmarks.

9

Adam, Eve, Tree, Apple, Serpent, Nakedness, Fig Leaf are all words that reside in the same neighborhood. In this case, the neighborhood is Genesis.

Genesis 3:6 tells how Eve ate the apple. Half of that sentence is visual and imaginable and links together like homes in a neighborhood. The other half represents no picture. Here's part of the verse. Circle the most memorable half.

This half   or   This half

Genesis 3:6 /   ... woman saw that the fruit of the tree was good...

The words <u>Genesis 3:6</u> creates no picture, but the other half does create a picture. Can you mentally see Eve looking and then reaching for the apple?

Our minds draws up the image. The image is like a movie being played out because the story can be visualized. It lands in the same neighborhood. It has a storyline fixed into our memory.

The word 'Genesis' and the numbers 3 & 6 do not have a storyline, thus making it difficult for it to settle into our minds. There's no shape, texture, and color to Genesis 3:6, as there is to the woman looking at the forbidden fruit.

It's the story within the verse we remember. It's seldom the other way around. It's similar to when we say, "I can picture his face, but I can't remember his name." Why so? The face is a visual, the name is not. Genesis 3:6 doesn't have a face, but keep reading, it will.

Exaggerations are memorable because they are ... exaggerated. It's the bizarre, the strange, the unusual, the absurd that we remember. Did you remember the car next to yours at the stop light? You would if it were shaped like a giant lamp on wheels.

The mundane things of everyday life are easy to forget. Do you recall what you ate for breakfast? Do you remember brushing your teeth?

Do you remember driving to work and seeing the sights on the way? Would you have remembered if a giraffe ran in front of your car? Do you think you would have forgotten if you had seen a train that flew like an airplane or an airplane that traveled like a train? Probably not.

We can stretch that exaggeration even more. Imagine seeing an elephant reading a book at the library or a giant book smoking a cigar. Those exaggerated images are memorable. When things are out of whack we never forget them.

The *VINE* system is going to help us to remember the Bible.

The next page lists the books of the Bible, while pages 26 - 41 wraps the *VINE* around them.

VISUALIZING THE BOOKS

The 66 Books of the Bible

Genesis	Nahum
Exodus	Habakkuk
Leviticus	Zephaniah
Numbers	Haggai
Deuteronomy	Zechariah
Joshua	Malachi
Judges	Matthew
Ruth	Mark
1 Samuel	Luke
2 Samuel	John
1 Kings	Acts
2 Kings	Romans
1 Chronicles	1 Corinthians
2 Chronicles	2 Corinthians
Ezra	Galatians
Nehemiah	Ephesians
Esther	Philippians
Job	Colossians
Psalms	1 Thessalonians
Proverbs	2 Thessalonians
Ecclesiastes	1 Timothy
Song of Solomon	2 Timothy
Isaiah	Titus
Jeremiah	Philemon
Lamentations	Hebrews
Ezekiel	James
Daniel	1 Peter
Hosea	2 Peter
Joel	1 John
Amos	2 John
Obadiah	3 John
Jonah	Jude
Micah	Revelation

Genesis ⟶ Genie Bottle

Exodus ⟶ Exit Sign

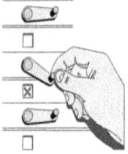

Leviticus ⟶ Ballot Lever

Numbers ⟶ Numb (Brrrr)

Deuteronomy ⟶ Dew from grass

Joshua ⟶ Jar

 Judges ⟶ Judge

 Ruth ⟶ Tooth

 1 Samuel ⟶ Uncle Sam's Hat

 2 Samuel ⟶ U.S. Flag

 1 Kings ⟶ King's Crown

 2 Kings ⟶ Chess Piece King

1 Chronicles ⟶ Newsboy

2 Chronicles ⟶ Newspaper

Ezra ⟶ Snake (sssss-ra)

Nehemiah ⟶ Knee

Esther ⟶ Ether Mask

Job ⟶ Jackhammer on the Job

Psalms —————————→ Palm

Proverbs —————————→ Provolone Cheese

Ecclesiastes —————————→ Escalator

Song of Solomon —————————→ Choir Singing

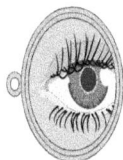

Isaiah —————————→ Eye

Jeremiah —————————→ Bullfrog

 Lamentations ⟶ Lemon

 Ezekiel ⟶ E Z Chair

 Daniel ⟶ Dandelion

 Hosea ⟶ Hose

 Joel ⟶ Jail

 Amos ⟶ Aim

Obadiah ──────────► Bed

Jonas ──────────► Phone

Micah ──────────► Microphone

Nahum ──────────► Neigh from Horse

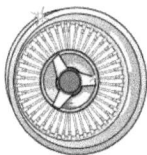

Habakkuk ──────────► Hubcap

Zephaniah ──────────► Zipper

Haggai   ⟶   Hugging

Zechariah   ⟶   Sack

Malachi   ⟶   Malt

Matthew   ⟶   Mat

Mark   ⟶   On your Mark

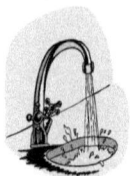

Luke   ⟶   Luke Warm

John ⟶ Toilet Paper

Acts ⟶ Stage

Romans ⟶ Roman Soldier

1 Corinthians ⟶ Apple (Core)

2 Corinthians ⟶ Core

Galatians ⟶ Gallon of Milk

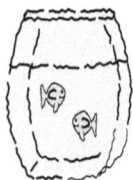

Ephesians —————▶ Fish

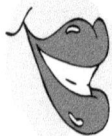

Philippians —————▶ Full Lip

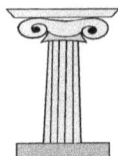

Colossians —————▶ Column

1 Thessalonians —————▶ Salon Hairdryer

2 Thessalonians —————▶ Scissors at Salon

1 Timothy —————▶ Timber

2 Timothy ⟶ Cutting Timber

Titus ⟶ Tightrope

Philemon ⟶ Fill 'er up

Hebrews ⟶ Brewed Coffee

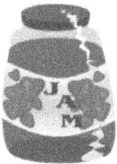

James ⟶ Jam

1 Peter ⟶ Pistol Pete

2 Peter ⟶ Peterbilt Truck

1 John ⟶ Outhouse (1 Moon)

2 John ⟶ Tub (2 Handles)

3 John ⟶ Razor (3 dials)

Jude ⟶ Judo

Revelation ⟶ Revolving Door

Each book of the Bible has been translated to a visual. Spend a few minutes reviewing the pictures that represent each book.

The following pages will weave the pictures together into a story creating imagery, neighborhoods, and exaggeration. The *VINE* system will be complete.

Put yourself into the story and let your imagination loose. Then, take the quizzes and be surprised. You've just memorized the 66 Books of the Bible.

A GENIE, EXITING his bottle to vote, pulls the LEVER with his cold NUMB hand for Mr. Snowman.

(Genesis, Exodus, Leviticus, Numbers)

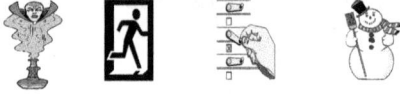

Snowmen are scooping up DEW on the ground using a JAR. The jar, used by JUDGES as a gavel, breaks and hits their TOOTH in a RUTH-less fashion.

(Deuteronomy, Joshua, Judges, Ruth)

The tooth flies into UNCLE SAM's hat and onto UNCLE SAM's flag, then into all the KINGS men, both of them. The incident is reported in FIRST CHRONICLES and SECOND CHRONICLES throughout the country.

(1 Samuel, 2 Samuel, 1 Kings, 2 Kings,
1 Chronicles, 2 Chronicles)

Review

Rearrange the first 14 Books of the Bible in order

_____	2 Samuel
_____	Deuteronomy
_____	Ruth
_____	1 Chronicles
_____	Joshua
_____	1 Samuel
_____	1 Kings
_____	Leviticus
_____	2 Chronicles
_____	Judges
_____	Exodus
_____	2 Kings
_____	Genesis
_____	Numbers

Suddenly, appearing from under the newspapers is a SNAKE making a SISSING sound, *EZZZRA*. The snake begins to wrap itself around a man's KNEE who faints. Doctors apply ETHER to keep him still, but the sound of the loud JACKHAMMERS from the job site outside his window help to revive him.

(Ezra, Nehemiah, Esther, Job)

The jackhammer is hammering into a PALM covered with PROVOLONE cheese. The cheese spills onto an ESCALATOR as the CHOIR is SINGING its praise with EYEBALLS fixed on this strange scene, including that of a very large bullfrog, named JEREMIAH.

**(Psalms, Proverbs, Ecclesiastes,
Song of Solomon, Isaiah, Jeremiah)**

**NOTE: The choir has eyes, the eyeball is an eye and the bullfrog has big eyes.
This helps us to remember it's Song of Solomon, Isaiah, and Jeremiah.**

The bullfrog is sitting on a huge LEMON, then hops from lemon to lemon until it lands on an EZ BOY RECLINER. The recliner is covered with DANDELIONS until it's HOSED off.

(Lamentations, Ezekiel, Daniel, Hosea)

Review

Beginning with <u>Ezra</u>, place in order the next 14 Books of the Bible

_____	Lamentations
_____	Isaiah
_____	Daniel
_____	Song of Solomon
_____	Nehemiah
_____	Esther
_____	Jeremiah
_____	Job
_____	Ecclesiastes
_____	Hosea
_____	Ezra
_____	Psalms
_____	Ezekiel
_____	Proverbs

The hose is wrapped around the bars of a JAIL and can't get out until it shoots an ARROW at a target which opens the cell door.

Arrows stick into the BED with PHONES hiding underneath. Phones, set up as MICROPHONES, are being used by a horse who utters …*NA-HUM!*

(Joel, Amos, Obadiah, Jonah, Micah, Nahum)

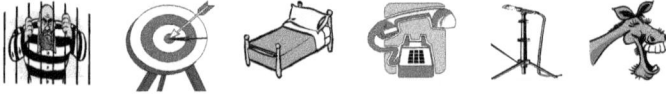

The horse is making so much noise that a huge HUBCAP is used to ZIP up the animal's mouth. The zippers are HUGGING because of their accomplishment. To stop them from hugging, a huge SACK is put over them and is later stuffed into a MALT.

(Habakkuk, Zephaniah, Haggai, Zechariah, Malachi)

NOTE: Hub Cap is one word (hubcap). It becomes one when hub and cap are zipped up. This reminds you that Zephaniah follows.

The malt shake is placed on a long MAT covering a track as runners begin to take their MARK. They slip because of the LUKE warm water on the surface. The race is postponed until toilet paper from a PORTAJOHN is used to wipe it up.

(Matthew, Mark, Luke, John)

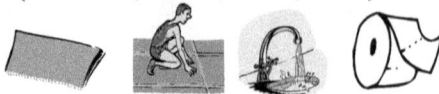

Review

Beginning with <u>Joel</u>, place in order the next 15 Books of the Bible

_____	Haggai
_____	Amos
_____	Zephaniah
_____	John
_____	Malachi
_____	Mark
_____	Obadiah
_____	Nahum
_____	Luke
_____	Zechariah
_____	Matthew
_____	Jonah
_____	Joel
_____	Habakkuk
_____	Micah

The rest of the toilet paper is used as curtains from a one ACT play performed by ROMANS who eat two giant apples, including the CORES and drink a GALLON of milk. To their surprise, they see FISH swimming inside the milk.

**(Acts, Romans, 1 Corinthians, 2 Corinthians,
Galatians, Ephesians)**

The fish, with FULL LIPS, say they want out. A tank is filled for them as decorative COLUMNS are placed inside for their enjoyment. Hanging from the columns is a HAIRDRYER and a PAIR of SCISSORS taken from the local SALON.

(Philippians, Colossians, 1 Thessalonians, 2 Thessalonians)

The scissors from the salon are used to cut down trees ... listen .. *TIMBER, TIMBER!* The log is being used as a tightrope. It's much easier to walk on than a rope, but more dangerous if it falls on the spectators below.

(1 Timothy, 2 Timothy, Titus)

<u>Review</u>

Beginning with <u>Acts</u>, place in order the next 13 Books of the Bible

_____	2 Thessalonians
_____	1 Timothy
_____	Galatians
_____	Titus
_____	1 Thessalonians
_____	Acts
_____	Colossians
_____	Ephesians
_____	2 Timothy
_____	Philippians
_____	1 Corinthians
_____	Romans
_____	2 Corinthians

The tightrope is being used to check the oil of a car which would indicate if more oil needs to be FILLED. Because no oil is available, BREWED coffee is added. The driver realizes this doesn't work and he JAMS on the brakes until the car PETERS and PETERS out

(Philemon, Hebrews, James, 1 Peter, 2 Peter)

As he makes his way to the john, 3 mechanics, all named JOHN, look over the engine. They give the car a JUDO chop and the car REVS up once again.

(1 John, 2 John, 3 John, Jude, Revelation)

NOTE: Even though some of the stories were different from the illustrations, (1 Peter to Revelation) it was easy to remember the link as each Book was connected to the next.

Review

Beginning with <u>Philemon</u>, place in order the remaining Books of the Bible

_____	1 Peter
_____	1 John
_____	Jude
_____	2 John
_____	James
_____	Hebrews
_____	Revelation
_____	3 John
_____	2 Peter
_____	Philemon

Review

A ***GENIE*** ***EXITS*** his bottle to vote and pulls the ***LEVER*** with his cold ***NUMB*** hand for Mr. Snowman.

Snowmen are scooping up ***DEW*** on the ground using a ***JAR***. The jar is used by ***JUDGES*** as a gavel. The broken glass breaks her ***TOOTH*** in a ***RUTH***-less fashion.

The tooth flies into ***UNCLE SAM'S*** hat and onto ***UNCLE SAM'S*** flag, then into all the ***KINGS*** men, both of them. The incident is reported in ***1 CHRONICLES*** and ***2 CHRONICLES***.

Genesis

Exodus

Leviticus

Numbers

Deuteronomy

Joshua

Judges

Ruth

1 Samuel

2 Samuel

1 Kings

2 Kings

1 Chronicles

2 Chronicles

Suddenly, appearing from under the newspapers is a snake making a sissing sound, **_EZRA_**. The snake begins to wrap itself around a man's **_KNEE_** who faints. Doctors apply **_ETHER_** to keep him still, but the sound of the loud **_JACKHAMMER_** from the job site outside his window help to revive him.

The jackhammer is hammering into a huge **_PALM_** covered with **_PROVOLONE_** cheese. The cheese spills onto an **_ESCALATOR_** surrounded by a choir **_SINGING_** its praise, as **_EYES_** are fixed on this strange scene, including that of a very large bullfrog, named **_JEREMIAH_**.

Ezra

Nehemiah

Esther

Job

Psalms

Proverbs

Ecclesiastes

Song of Solomon

Isaiah

Jeremiah

The bullfrog is sitting on a huge **LEMON**, then hops from lemon to lemon until it lands on an **EZ** BOY RECLINER. The recliner is covered with **DANDELIONS** until it's **HOSED** off.

The hose is wrapped around the bars of a **JAIL** and can't get out until it shoots and **AIMS** an arrow at a target which opens the cell door.

Arrows are stuck in the **BED** with **PHONES** hiding underneath. Phones, set up as **MICROPHONES**, are being used by a horse who utters **NAHUM**!

Lamentations

Ezekiel

Daniel

Hosea

Joel

Amos

Obadiah

Jonah

Micah

Nahum

The horse is making so much noise that a huge **_HUBCAP_** is used to **_ZIP_** up the animal's mouth. The zippers are **_HUGGING_** because of their accomplishment. To stop them from hugging a huge **_SACK_** is put over them and is later stuffed into a **_MALT_** shake.

The malt shake is placed on a long **_MAT_** covering a track as runners begin to take their **_MARK_**. They slip because of the **_LUKE_** warm water on the surface. The race is postponed until toilet paper from a **_JOHN_** is used to wipe up the water.

Habakkuk

Zephaniah

Haggai

Zechariah

Malachi

Matthew

Mark

Luke

John

The rest of the toilet paper is used as curtains from a one ***ACT*** play performed by ***ROMANS*** who eat two giant apples, including both ***CORES*** and drink a ***GALLON*** of milk. They are surprised seeing ***FISH*** swimming in the milk.

The fish, with ***FULL LIPS***, say they want out. A tank, filled for them with decorative ***COLUMNS,*** is placed inside for their enjoyment. Hanging from the columns is a ***HAIRDRYER*** and ***SCISSORS*** taken from the local ***SALON***.

Acts

Romans

1 Corinthians

2 Corinthians

Galatians

Ephesians

Philippians

Colossians

1 Thessalonians

2 Thessalonians

The scissors from the salon are used to cut down trees ... listen ..
TIMBER, TIMBER! The log is being used as a ***TIGHTROPE***. It's
much easier to walk on than a rope, but more dangerous if it falls on
the spectators below.

The tightrope is being used is check the oil of a car which would
indicate if more oil needs to be ***FILLED***. Because no oil is available,
BREWED coffee is added.

The driver realizes this doesn't work and he ***JAMS*** on the brakes until
the car ***PETERS*** and ***PETERS*** out. As he makes his way to the
JOHN, 3 mechanics, all named ***JOHN***, look over the engine. They
give the car a ***JUDO*** chop and the car ***REVS*** up once again.

1 Timothy

2 Timothy

Titus

Philemon

Hebrews

1 Peter

2 Peter

1 John

2 John

3 John

Judo

Revelation

From the list below, fill in the 7 Missing Books

Genesis ... Exodus ...

Leviticus	Psalms	Habakkuk	Colossians
Numbers	Proverbs	Zephaniah	1 Thessalonians
Deuteronomy	Ecclesiastes	Haggai	2 Thessalonians
Joshua	Song of Solomon		1 Timothy
Judges	Isaiah	Malachi	2 Timothy
	Jeremiah	Matthew	Titus
1 Samuel	Lamentations	Mark	Philemon
2 Samuel		Luke	
1 Kings	Daniel	John	James
2 Kings	Hosea		1 Peter
1 Chronicles	Joel	Romans	2 Peter
2 Chronicles	Amos	1 Corinthians	1 John
	Obadiah	2 Corinthians	2 John
Nehemiah	Jonah		3 John
Esther	Micah	Ephesians	Jude
Job	Nahum	Philippians	Revelation

VISUALIZING THE NUMBERS

When it comes to the Bible, Numbers is not just a book that follows Leviticus. Numbers are chapters and verses that fill the pages from Genesis to Revelation. Learning how to remember these numbers will save you valuable time so you can easily find a specific scripture.

Without a system numbers are very difficult to commit to memory. They do not form any memorable pattern. There's no texture, color, or life to numbers. By themselves numbers lack pizzazz.

The use of the phonetic alphabet is the vehicle that will take you to the promised land when committing numbers to memory. Developed hundreds of years ago, the phonetic alphabet codes numbers to letters thus creating vivid pictures in the process.

There is no better system in recalling numbers than the phonetic alphabet system.

The Phonetic Alphabet

The 10 digits are coded to 10 consonant sounds. The sound of that letter will aid us in remembering the number.

0 is represented by the letters z, soft c, and s. Notice when you pronounce words with those sounds your teeth are clenched. The words Zoo, Center and Salad begin with the *sissing* sound.

1 is represented by the letters t and d. Those two letters produce the same sound. Notice the position of your tongue when you begin to say words as: David, Tony, Toledo and Denver.

2 is represented by the letter n. There's no other sound like the *N*. Words such as, Neck, Needle and kNife begin with your tongue pressed to the roof of your mouth.

3 is represented by the letter m. Your lips are together when you begin to say, Mother, Minnesota and Memory.

4 is represented by the letter r. Note the setup of your lips and tongue when you pronounce words such as: Rye, Reach and Rain.

5 is represented by the letter L. Notice the position of your tongue when you utter words like, Leader, Lovely and Law.

6 is represented by the letter j, soft g, sh, and ch. Words such as: Joy, George, SHare and CHurch all start with your lips puckered.

7 is represented by the letters k, hard g, hard c, and q. The *KA* sound equals the number 7. Words such as: Kettle, Card, Girl and Quick begin with the same sound.

8 is represented by the letters f, v, and ph. Your lips are close together when you utter the words, Ferry, Velvet and PHone.

9 is represented by the letters p and b. The popping sounds of Park, Pal, Bake and Boo equals the number 9.

10 digits are replaced by 10 consonant sounds.

0 = z, soft c, and **s.** As a reminder...Zero ends with **O.**
Examples of words that are coded to the number 0.
ice...has...is...was...haze...sew...so...icy...use

1 = t and **d.** As a reminder...the letters *t* and *d* stand on 1 leg.
Examples...
tie...die...dye...head...wood...hat...wet...ate...hot

2 = n. As a reminder...the letter *n* stands on 2 legs.
Examples...
win...in...on...Noah...wine...when...hen...honey...no

3 = m. as a reminder...the letter *m* stands on 3 legs or the 3M Co.
Examples...
Ma...ham...home...me...May...mow...yam...moo...my

4 = r. As a reminder...the number Fou**r** ends with *R.*
Examples...
rye...oar...ore...or...hire...hour...hair...our...row

5 = L. As a reminder...roman numeral 50 is L.
Examples...
law...eel...wheel...lay...low...hole...heel...ale...Lou

6 = j, soft g, sh, and **ch.** As a reminder...mirror image of 6 resembles j.
Examples...
wage...chew...ash...jay...show...shoe...wish...Joe...age

7 = k, hard c and **g, q.** As a reminder...a backwards 7 makes up k.
Examples...
key...go...Kay...wick...egg...queue...cue...hack...wig

8 = f, v, and **ph.** As a reminder...a written *f* resembles an 8.
Examples...
heave...have...if...ivy...of...foe...wife...wave...half

9 = p and **b.** As a reminder...a mirror image of *p* resembles a 9.
Examples...
pie...hope...hip...pay...bee...be...hoop...up...bye

Remember, the letters *a, e, i, o, u, w, h,* and *y* have no value. They help to set up words.

The letters *th* have no value when together, such as *thou, they* and *the.* The *th* sound is slightly different than the *t* and *d* sound.

You don't have to be a good speller. It's the sound we are after. *Knife* is pronounced *nife*, as we hear only the letters *n* and *f*. *Knife* represents 28, not 728. *Tough* equals 18, because it's pronounced *TuF*. *Rough* is 48, because it's pronounced *RuF*. *Dough* is 1, because it's pronounced *Doe*. Only the *d* sound is heard.

Double letters count as one. Su*mm*er = 034, not 0334. Bu*tt*er is 914, not 9114. However, the word "accentuate" is 70261, because it's pronounced aK-CeN-CHew-aTe.

The letter *X* equals 70. *Box* is pronounced *boKS*.

TION equals 62, as in opera*tion*, na*tion*, and ova*tion*.

TCH equals 6 because it's a quick *ch* sound, such as i*tch*, scra*tch* and wa*tch*.

DG equals 6, as in fu*DG*e, ju*DG*e, and e*DG*e.

CK equals 7, not 77. Words such as, ba*CK*, lo*CK*, and sna*CK* have the AK sound. A hard *k* represents the number 7.

A number preceded by a zero avoids confusion with single digit numbers. For instance, 1:25 is TuNNeL, while 12:5 is written as 12:05 (ToNSiL).

Keep in mind ...

It's the **SOUND** that counts

Putting it all together

The following pages list every chapter and verse of the Bible.

By applying the *VINE* system, discussed on pages 6 - 11, you'll be able to remember any passage of the Bible.

For example, Genesis 9:11. Genesis is represented by a Genie bottle; 911 translates to PoTaTo. The scripture is about God saying never again will a flood destroy the earth.

Now it's time to combine *Genie* bottle, *Potato* and *Flood* into one story. Visualizing a Genie throwing potatoes into the floodwaters will tell you where to find the passage about God flooding the earth.

Imagining Genies and potatoes will help, not hinder, you in remembering the passage. Your natural memory will know that God did not flood the earth with potatoes. You'll know the difference.

Find keys words in a passage and combine the picture of the book with the word or phrase beside the verse. Use your imagination to create vivid pictures.

If you visualize getting on your MARK and racing to SUPPER, but finding a TRaiToR at the table, you'll always know where to find the scripture about 'The Last Supper." Mark, 14:14.

The Bible has taken on another dimension as the Books, Chapters, Verses, and Scripture have been developed into pictures.

Take the time to know the phonetic alphabet, and with your Bible nearby, let your imagination run wild. It will be an unforgettable ride.

A recap of the Phonetic Alphabet.

$$0 = \quad \text{s, z, soft c,}$$
$$1 = \quad \text{t, d}$$
$$2 = \quad \text{n}$$
$$3 = \quad \text{m}$$
$$4 = \quad \text{r}$$
$$5 = \quad \text{L}$$
$$6 = \quad \text{sh, ch, j, soft g}$$
$$7 = \quad \text{k, q, hard c/g}$$
$$8 = \quad \text{f, v, ph}$$
$$9 = \quad \text{p, b}$$

For more answers on the uses of the phonetic alphabet,
Be sure and read Page 78 following this section

The Rules

Like everything in life, there are rules to follow. Here are a dozen to stay on course for remembering numbers:

- Ten digits are replaced by ten consonant sounds to make words.

- The vowels, *a, e, i, o, u*, as well as *w, h, y* are not coded to any letter. They're used as fillers.

- The letters *th*, when together, have no value, such as **th**ou, and **th**e. The sound is slightly different than the *t* and *d* sound.

- You need not be a good speller. It's the sound that matters. Therefore, the word, *k**n**i**f**e* translates to only 2 and 8, instead of 7 2 8, because the letter *k* is silent.

- The letter **x** equals the number 70. **X** is pronounced e**KS**, because *k* equals 7 and *s* equals 0.

- Double letters count as one. **Su**mm**e**r codes to 034, not 0334. **Bu**tt**e**r is 914, not 9114. However, the word, *accent* is 7021, because it's pronounced a**K**-**C**e**NT**.

- *Tion* equals 62, as in opera**tion** (opera-**shun**), na**tion** (na-**shun**), and ova**tion** (o-va-**shun**).

- *Tch* equals 6 because it's a quick *ch* sound, such as i**tch**, ha**tch**, wi**tch**, and wa**tch**.

- *Dg* equals 6, as in fu**dg**e, ju**dg**e, and e**dg**e.

- *Ck* equals 7, not 77. Words such as wha**ck**, hi**ck**, and ho**ck**ey have the *ak* sound. A hard *k* represents the number 7.

- Tough equals 18, because it's pronounced **tuf**. **Rough** is 48, whereas **D**ough is 1, because it's pronounced **d**oe.

- Learn this system. It will change your life.

1:1 Dad	1:47 truck	2:13 anytime	2:59 no help
1:2 tuna	1:48 driveway	2:14 under	2:60 nachos
1:3 dime	1:49 trap	2:15 needle	2:61 inched
1:4 door	1:50 dolls	2:16 window wash	2:62 nation
1:5 tail	1:51 tilt	2:17 antique	2:63 no shame
1:6 dish	1:52 ate alone	2:18 hand off	2:64 unsure
1:7 dog	1:53 tell me	2:19 no top	2:65 in jail
1:8 TV	1:54 taller	2:20 onions	2:66 enjoy the show
1:9 tub	1:55 tell all	2:21 new window	2:67 unshake
1:10 toads	1:56 wet leash	2:22 an onion	2:68 inch off
1:11 deadwood	1:57 wet log	2:23 no name	2:69 inch by
1:12 hot town	1:58 tea leaf	2:24 no winner	2:70 knocks
1:13 daytime	1:59 tulip	2:25 any nail	3:1 mud
1:14 detour	1:60 dishes	2:26 an inch	3:2 money
1:15 title	1:61 touched	2:27 winning	3:3 mummy
1:16 hot dish	1:62 wet chin	2:28 new knife	3:4 hammer
1:17 hot dog	1:63 teach me	2:29 onion pie	3:5 mail
1:18 white dove	1:64 teacher	2:30 names	3:6 match
1:19 hot tip	1:65 touch wall	2:31 inmate	3:7 hammock
1:20 tennis	1:66 touch shoe	2:32 honeymoon	3:8 movie
1:21 tent	1:67 touch wig	2:33 no Mom	3:9 map
1:22 white onion	1:68 de ja vu	2:34 no more	3:10 mitts
1:23 denim	1:69 touch up	2:35 animal	3:11 matted
1:24 toner	1:70 dogs	2:36 no match	3:12 mitten
1:25 tunnel	1:71 ticket	2:37 new hammock	3:13 medium
1:26 teenage	1:72 taken	2:38 new movie	3:14 motor
1:27 tank	1:73 Tacoma	2:39 new map	3:15 motel
1:28 hide knife	1:74 taker	2:40 honors	3:16 my dish
1:29 tune up	1:75 tackle	2:41 honored	3:17 medic
1:30 dimes	1:76 dog show	2:42 no rain	3:18 midwife
1:31 tomato	1:77 hot cocoa	2:43 no room	3:19 made up
1:32 time in	1:78 hot coffee	2:44 in her hair	3:20 mayonnaise
1:33 time me	1:79 teacup	2:45 unreal	3:21 mint
1:34 terror	1:80 TV's	2:46 energy	3:22 ham, onion
1:35 oatmeal	2:1 window	2:47 New York	3:23 my name
1:36 dumb show	2:2 onion	2:48 nerve	3:24 minor
1:37 atomic	2:3 enemy	2:49 unwrap	3:25 monthly
1:38 time off	2:4 owner	2:50 nails	3:26 munch
1:39 tempo	2:5 nail	2:51 knelt	3:27 monkey
1:40 tires	2:6 notch	2:52 nylon	3:28 mean wife
1:41 tired	2:7 neck	2:53 only me	3:29 mean boy
1:42 train	2:8 knife	2:54 only her	3:30 Moms
1:43 drum	2:9 knob	2:55 Honolulu	3:31 homemade
1:44 terrier	2:10 nets	2:56 unleash	3:32 my man
1:45 trail	2:11 knotted	2:57 unlucky	3:33 my Mom
1:46 trash	2:12 Indian	2:58 only half	3:34 memory

3:35 home meal	4:15 rattle	5:7 leg	6:6 judge
3:36 my match	4:16 radish	5:8 leaf	6:7 shake
3:37 mimic	4:17 red wig	5:9 elbow	6:8 chef
3:38 home movie	4:18 write off	5:10 lettuce	6:9 ship
3:39 my map	4:19 wiretap	5:11 low tide	6:10 jets
3:40 hammers	4:20 rinse	5:12 Aladdin	6:11 cheated
3:41 mart	4:21 warrant	5:13 yell time	6:12 showtune
3:42 homerun	4:22 reunion	5:14 ladder	6:13 show time
3:43 my room	4:23 rename	5:15 ladle	6:14 ashtray
3:44 mirror	4:24 runner	5:16 late show	6:15 huge tail
3:45 moral	4:25 re-nail	5:17 late walk	6:16 huge dish
3:46 march	4:26 ranch	5:18 loud wife	6:17 huge dog
3:47 mark	4:27 ring	5:19 let up	6:18 showed off
3:48 I'm rough	4:28 run off	5:20 lions	6:19 showed up
3:49 more pie	4:29 run by	5:21 walnut	6:20 Chinese
3:50 malice	4:30 rooms	5:22 linen	6:21 giant
3:51 melt	4:31 roomed	5:23 yell enemy	6:22 John Wayne
3:52 melon	4:32 Roman	5:24 liner	6:23 huge name
3:53 I'm lame	4:33 our Mom	5:25 lonely	6:24 January
3:54 mailer	4:34 rumor	5:26 lunch	6:25 channel
3:55 mail all	4:35 airmail	5:27 long	6:26 change
3:56 mulch	4:36 rematch	5:28 yellow knife	6:27 junk
3:57 milk	4:37 remake	5:29 line up	6:28 huge knife
3:58 mail off	4:38 war movie	5:30 limes	6:29 chin up
3:59 my lip	4:39 ramp	5:31 yell - mad	6:30 jams
3:60 matches	4:40 roars	5:32 lemon	6:31 chimed
3:61 machete	4:41 reread	5:33 hello Mom	6:32 chimney
3:62 machine	4:42 rerun	5:34 yell more	6:33 show Mom
3:63 my shame	4:43 our room	5:35 lame wheel	6:34 wash my hair
3:64 major	4:44 hear the roar	5:36 I'll match you	6:35 huge mall
3:65 match well	4:45 hear her yell	5:37 yellow mug	6:36 huge match
3:66 I'm the judge	4:46 you're rich	5:38 I'll move	6:37 jam key
4:1 rod	4:47 rework	5:39 lamp	6:38 show movie
4:2 rain	4:48 you're rough	5:40 walrus	6:39 shampoo
4:3 ram	4:49 rare buy	5:41 Lord	6:40 chairs
4:4 rear	4:50 rolls	5:42 learn	6:41 shirt
4:5 rail	4:51 world	5:43 yellow room	6:42 journey
4:6 roach	4:52 hairline	5:44 lower hair	6:43 germ
4:7 rug	4:53 realm	5:45 lower wheel	6:44 huge rear
4:8 roof	4:54 roller	5:46 allergy	6:45 cheer - yell
4:9 rope	5:1 wallet	5:47 yellow rug	6:46 church
4:10 roads	5:2 lion	6:1 shed	6:47 shark
4:11 rooted	5:3 lamb	6:2 chain	6:48 sheriff
4:12 routine	5:4 lawyer	6:3 gym	6:49 cherry pie
4:13 redeem	5:5 lily	6:4 chair	6:50 shoelace
4:14 radar	5:6 leash	6:5 jail	6:51 child

6:52 huge lion	7:17 catwalk	7:64 catcher	8:21 faint
6:53 huge lime	7:18 get off	7:65 catch well	8:22 heavy onion
6:54 jewelry	7:19 get up	7:66 catch show	8:23 venom
6:55 huge lily	7:20 wagons	7:67 hockey check	8:24 funny hair
6:56 huge leash	7:21 candy	7:68 catch a wave	8:25 vinyl
6:57 chilly week	7:22 cannon	7:69 ketchup	8:26 finish
6:58 chilly eve	7:23 economy	7:70 cookies	8:27 funky
6:59 huge lip	7:24 canary	7:71 kicked	8:28 funny wife
6:60 judges	7:25 canal	7:72 cocoon	8:29 heavy nap
6:61 judged	7:27 king	7:73 kick me	8:30 famous
6:62 huge ocean	7:28 weak Navy	7:74 Quaker	8:31 foamed
6:63 judge him	7:29 canopy	7:75 giggle	8:32 famine
6:64 wash ashore	7:30 combs	7:76 quick show	8:33 I have a Mommy
6:65 huge jail	7:31 comet	7:77 cakewalk	8:34 foamier
6:66 show judge	7:32 common	7:78 kickoff	8:35 family
6:67 huge check	7:33 comb me	7:79 cake, pie	8:36 heavy match
6:68 huge chef	7:34 comb hair	7:80 caves	8:37 heavy mug
6:69 huge ship	7:35 camel	7:81 coughed	8:38 have my half
6:70 jacuzzi	7:36 game show	7:82 coffin	8:39 have my pie
6:71 jacket	7:37 comic	7:83 give me	8:40 fires
6:72 chicken	7:38 game off	7:84 caviar	8:41 fried
6:73 chew gum	7:39 camp	7:85 gavel	8:42 frown
6:74 sugar	7:40 cars	7:86 go fish	8:43 farm
6:75 juggle	7:41 karate	7:87 hockey fake	8:44 fire her
6:76 huge catch	7:42 green	7:88 give off	8:45 farewell
6:77 Chicago	7:43 cream	7:89 give up	8:46 fresh
6:78 shake off	7:44 career	8:1 feet	8:47 frog
6:79 check up	7:45 grill	8:2 phone	8:48 very heavy
6:80 shaves	7:46 crash	8:3 foam	8:49 frappe
6:81 shoved	7:47 crack	8:4 fire	8:50 falls
7:1 cat	7:48 grave	8:5 file	8:51 flat
7:2 gun	7:49 grape	8:6 fish	8:52 violin
7:3 gum	7:50 calls	8:7 fog	8:53 flame
7:4 car	7:51 colt	8:8 fife	8:54 flower
7:5 eagle	7:52 clown	8:9 FBI	8:55 follow all
7:6 coach	7:53 clam	8:10 fads	8:56 foliage
7:7 cake	7:54 clear	8:11 photo ID	8:57 flag
7:8 coffee	7:55 kill a whale	8:12 half ton	8:58 fluff
7:9 cup	7:56 clash	8:13 feed me	8:59 flip
7:10 cats	7:57 clock	8:14 fatter	8:60 fishes
7:11 cadet	7:58 glove	8:15 fiddle	8:61 fished
7:12 kitten	7:59 clip	8:16 fetish	8:62 fusion
7:13 academy	7:60 coaches	8:17 vodka	8:63 fetch him
7:14 guitar	7:61 cashed	8:18 feet off	8:64 fish here
7:15 cattle	7:62 cushion	8:19 fed up	8:65 heavy shell
7:16 cottage	7:63 catch me	8:20 fence	8:66 a heavy judge

53

9:1 bat	9:47 break	10:31 eats meat	11:25 wet toe nail
9:2 bone	9:48 proof	10:32 that's a woman	11:26 tighten shoe
9:3 bomb	9:49 prop	10:33 Idaho's my home	11:27 Titanic
9:4 bear	9:50 pillows	10:34 eats more	11:28 date on/off
9:5 ball	9:51 plate	10:35 decimal	11:29 had a tune-up
9:6 beach	9:52 plane	10:36 ate so much	11:30 dead mouse
9:7 bike	9:53 bloom	10:37 that's my guy	11:31 dead meat
9:8 puff	9:54 player	10:38 that's my wife	11:32 dead man
9:9 pipe	9:55 pool hall	10:39 wet swamp	11:33 eat at my home
9:10 boathouse	9:56 blush	10:40 tweezers	11:34 hit timer
9:11 potato	9:57 black	10:41 dessert	11:35 eat oatmeal
9:12 button	9:58 bluff	10:42 it's rainy	11:36 too, too much
9:13 bottom	9:59 apple pie	10:43 disarm	11:37 today muggy
9:14 butter	9:60 bushes	10:44 it's a horror	11:38 do eat my half
9:15 battle	9:61 pushed	10:45 eat cereal	11:39 hot Tampa
9:16 paid wage	9:62 passion	10:46 it's rich	11:40 detours
9:17 paddock	10:1 test	10:47 it's rocky	11:41 dehydrate
9:18 paid off	10:2 tow away zone	10:48 it's rough	11:42 wide turn
9:19 paid up	10:3 days home	10:49 disrobe	11:43 daydream
9:20 bones	10:4 dizzier	10:50 tassels	11:44 what a terror
9:21 paint	10:5 tassel	10:51 disallowed	11:45 hot trail
9:22 banana	10:6 dosage	10:52 twice alone	11:46 out with trash
9:23 buy new home	10:7 desk	11:01 dead city	11:47 tow truck
9:24 pioneer	10:8 dizzy wife	11:02 die too soon	11:48 hot driveway
9:25 penny well	10:9 day spa	11:03 dates me	11:49 tightrope
9:26 punch	10:10 wet seeds	11:04 today's weather	11:50 details
9:27 hopping	10:11 tested	11:05 wet tassel	11:51 detailed
9:28 buy a knife	10:12 Dizzy Dean	11:06 Dad's watch	11:52 dateline
9:29 pin up	10:13 toast him	11:07 today is OK	11:53 dead limb
9:30 poems	10:14 hot cider	11:08 date is off	11:54 weed tiller
9:31 bombed	10:15 wet saddle	11:09 heated soup	11:55 dead lily
9:32 pay money	10:16 taste shoe	11:10 eat toads	11:56 wet daily wash
9:33 pay Mom	10:17 wet sidewalk	11:11 outdated	11:57 deadlock
9:34 balmy weather	10:18 woodstove	11:12 hit titan	12:01 twin city
9:35 pay me all	10:19 heats it up	11:13 dead time	12:03 a tiny sum
9:36 pay my wage	10:20 it's noisy	11:14 dated her	12:04 dinosaur
9:37 pay my week	10:21 disowned	11:15 do detail	12:05 tonsil
9:38 pay me half	10:22 it's neon	11:16 hot, hot dish	12:06 twins age
9:39 pump	10:23 it's on me	11:17 dead dog	12:07 tiny sock
9:40 press	10:24 it's on her	11:18 dead dove	12:08 twin sofa
9:41 port	10:25 it's on the wall	11:19 heat hot tub	12:09 tunes up
9:42 brown	10:26 it's in the wash	11:20 titans	12:10 doughnuts
9:43 broom	10:27 tossing	11:21 dead end	12:11 dented
9:44 barrier	10:28 it's in the ivy	11:22 hid white onion	12:12 downtown
9:45 prowl	10:29 it's in the pie	11:23 titanium	12:13 Tiny Tim
9:46 brush	10:30 dismiss	11:24 eat dinner	12:14 wet winter

12:15 hot handle	13:02 time is now	13:48 dome roof	14:35 dry meal
12:16 tiny dish	13:03 hit the museum	13:49 hid my ruby	14:36 dry match
12:17 tan dog	13:04 do you miss her	13:50 dumb laws	14:37 dry mug
12:18 attentive	13:05 hid the missile	13:51 dim light	14:38 dream off
12:19 don't buy	13:06 time his wash	13:52 tame lion	14:39 tramp
12:20 eat onions	13:07 tummy sick	13:53 hot meal - ham	14:40 terrors
12:21 tenant	13:08 hide my safe	13:54 hit molar	14:41 try hard
12:22 tiny Nun	13:09 eat my soup	13:55 dumb oil well	14:42 dry run
12:23 tiny name	13:10 timeouts	13:56 hid my eyelash	14:43 dry arm
12:24 tiny honor	13:11 demoted	13:57 time log	14:44 dry your hair
12:25 down the Nile	13:12 wet mitten	13:58 dumb love	14:45 true, really
12:26 tiny notch	13:13 dumb dumb	13:59 oatmeal pie	14:46 terror watch
12:27 tanning	13:14 diameter	14:01 trust	14:47 tire wreck
12:28 twin knife	13:15 timidly	14:02 treason	14:48 dry her off
12:29 tiny knob	13:16 heat my dish	14:03 dries him	14:49 tore, rip
12:30 tan moose	13:17 automatic	14:04 dresser	14:50 trials
12:31 dynamite	13:18 hit my TV	14:05 drizzle	14:51 derailed
12:32 tinman	13:19 timid boy	14:06 dressage	14:52 water lawn
12:33 tiny Mummy	13:20 demons	14:07 to the rescue	14:53 tree limb
12:34 eat no more	13:21 diamond	14:08 dries off	14:54 trailer
12:35 eat no meal	13:22 dominion	14:09 tree sap	14:55 drill wall
12:36 twin match	13:23 hate my name	14:10 treats	14:56 door latch
12:37 dynamic	13:24 demeanor	14:11 traded	14:57 trail walk
12:38 twin movie	13:25 do women wail	14:12 trade in	14:58 true love
12:39 tone me up	13:26 hide my nacho	14:13 Dartmouth	14:59 wet ear lobe
12:40 dinners	13:27 timing	14:14 trader	14:60 trashes
12:41 Tony Award	13:28 dummy knife	14:15 turtle	14:61 trash it
12:42 tune her in	13:29 do men obey	14:16 dry dish	14:62 duration
12:43 tiny room	13:30 hide my mouse	14:17 dry dock	14:63 dear chum
12:44 dinnerware	13:31 teammate	14:18 trade off	14:64 dry chair
12:45 wooden rail	13:32 dumb man	14:19 dirty boy	14:65 dry jail
12:46 tiny rash	13:33 time my Mom	14:20 trains	14:66 Dear Judge
12:47 tiny rug	13:34 tame my hair	14:21 Toronto	14:67 try a shake
12:48 tin roof	13:35 hid my mail	14:22 dry onion	14:68 true chef
12:49 tiny rope	13:36 time my wash	14:23 train them	14:69 trash up
12:50 tunnels	13:37 time my walk	14:24 trainer	14:70 teargas
12:51 tiny wallet	13:38 dumb movie	14:25 drain well	14:71 target
12:52 dine alone	13:39 dim my hope	14:26 drench	14:72 dragon
12:53 tiny limb	13:40 timers	14:27 drink	15:01 deal set
12:54 tan lawyer	13:41 demerit	14:28 attorney fee	15:02 dials in
12:55 tiny lily	13:42 time the run	14:29 doorknob	15:03 tails him
12:56 tiny leash	13:43 heat my room	14:30 drums	15:04 Dolly's here
12:57 wooden leg	13:44 admirer	14:31 doormat	15:05 till soil
12:58 tiny leaf	13:45 admiral	14:32 doorman	15:06 dials shoe
12:59 tiny lip	13:46 hot mirage	14:33 Dear Mom	15:07 white Alaska
13:01 die, homicide	13:47 hit the mark	14:34 drummer	15:08 tells off

15:09 dials up	15:55 tall oil well	16:37 teach my guy	17:21 eat candy
15:10 toilets	15:56 it will latch	16:38 touch him off	17:22 take onion
15:11 diluted	15:57 daily log	16:39 hide the shampoo	17:23 taken home
15:12 dial tone	15:58 tall leaf	16:40 teachers	17:24 attack owner
15:13 tell it, Ma	15:59 hotel lobby	16:41 T shirt	17:25 wet canal
15:14 tall door	15:60 delicious	16:42 hot journey	17:26 attack Nashua
15:15 tall tale	15:61 tally sheet	16:43 had a germ	17:27 digging
15:16 tall dish	15:62 hotel chain	16:44 touch rear	17:28 attack the Navy
15:17 tall dog	15:63 tall chum	16:45 teach her well	17:29 take a nap
15:18 tall TV	15:63 tall chum	16:46 white church	17:30 take my house
15:19 teletype	16:01 digest	16:47 dish rag	17:31 take me out
15:20 daily news	16:02 touch the sun	16:48 hit sheriff	17:32 take me in
15:21 talent	16:03 touches him	16:49 hot cherry pie	17:33 take me home
15:22 wet linen	16:04 touches her	16:50 wet shells	17:34 tug my hair
15:23 tell on him	16:05 teach us well	16:51 touch wallet	17:35 take the mail
15:24 tell on her	16:06 dishes wash	16:52 eat chili now	17:36 take the match
15:25 tall nail	16:07 teach us, OK	16:53 touch limb	17:37 take mug
15:26 eat lunch	16:08 touch sofa	16:54 teach a lawyer	17:38 take me off
15:27 dialing	16:09 touches up	16:55 wet shallow well	17:39 take me up
15:28 hotel knife	16:10 wet sheets	16:56 touch eyelash	17:40 degrees
15:29 hot line up	16:11 dish it out	16:57 touch leg	17:41 ID card
15:30 tell him so	16:12 touchdown	16:58 touch lava	17:42 take a run
15:31 deli meat	16:13 it shot him	16:59 touch lip	17:43 diagram
15:32 tall man	16:14 white shutter	16:60 touch shoes	17:44 tag rear
15:33 tell Mom	16:15 dish towel	16:61 touch a jet	17:45 heat grill
15:34 tall hammer	16:16 touch dish	16:62 had a shoe shine	17:46 at car show
15:35 it will mellow	16:17 touch dog	16:63 touch a chime	17:47 wet creek
15:36 it will match	16:18 touch TV	17:01 tuxedo	17:48 autograph
15:37 tall mic	16:19 touch it up	17:02 hit casino	17:49 take her up
15:38 tell him off	16:20 touch nose	17:04 dogs her	17:50 tackles
15:39 hot lamp	16:21 hid giant	17:05 white castle	17:51 white cloud
15:40 tellers	16:22 touch onion	17:06 dog switch	17:52 hide clown
15:41 tall award	16:23 teach in Omaha	17:07 toxic	17:53 eat a clam
15:42 it will rain	16:24 teach in Rio	17:08 takes off	17:54 tickler
15:43 hotel room	16:25 teach in L.A.	17:09 duck soup	17:55 tickle all
15:44 taller oar	16:26 white shiny shoe	17:10 tickets	17:56 dog leash
15:45 it will roll	16:27 touching	17:11 dictate	17:57 white cloak
15:46 it will reach	16:28 touch knife	17:12 take down	17:58 white glove
15:47 it will rock	16:29 touch knob	17:13 dog team	18:01 TV set
15:48 tell her off	16:30 touch a moose	17:14 doctor	18:02 TV is on
15:49 Delaware Bay	16:31 touch my head	17:15 dog tail	18:03 TV zoom
15:50 it will lose	16:32 teach me now	17:16 dog dish	18:04 tough sir
15:51 tall load	16:33 teach Mom	17:17 tick tock	18:05 hide fossil
15:52 tall lion	16:34 touch my hair	17:18 talkative	18:06 TV switch
15:53 tall lamb	16:35 touch the mail	17:19 tack it up	18:07 TV is sick
15:54 tell a lawyer	16:36 touch my shoe	17:20 Dickens	18:08 TV is off

18:09 tough soap	19:31 tie up meat	20:26 noisy nacho	21:23 need a name
18:10 divots	19:32 tie up man	20:27 unsung	21:24 no dinner
18:11 divided	19:33 tie up Mom	20:28 niece / nephew	21:25 in denial
18:12 out of town	19:34 dip more	20:29 nice nap	21:26 Indian shoe
18:13 dive team	19:35 tie up mail	20:30 noisy mouse	21:27 knitting
18:14 tough tire	19:36 top match	20:31 noisy maid	21:28 need a knife
18:15 TV dial	19:37 tip mug	20:32 insomnia	21:29 antenna up
18:16 divide wash	19:38 top movie	20:33 nosy Mom	21:30 need my house
18:17 Daffy Duck	19:39 heat pump	20:34 owns more	21:31 handmade
18:44 tough roar	19:40 depress	20:35 nice meal	21:32 handyman
18:45 dive - roll	19:41 tea party	20:36 nice match	21:33 I need Mom
18:46 hot, fresh	19:42 white - brown	20:37 no smog	21:34 nightmare
18:47 wet frog	19:43 tapeworm	20:38 nice movie	21:35 windmill
18:48 tougher half	19:44 hit barrier	20:39 in a swamp	21:36 need much
18:49 eat free pie	19:45 top rail	20:40 nice raise	21:37 nutmeg
18:50 devils	19:46 white brush	20:41 nice hairdo	21:38 no time off
19:01 deposit	19:47 wet park	20:42 nice rain	21:39 in Tampa
19:02 eat poison	19:48 deprive	20:43 newsroom	21:40 undress
19:03 tips him	19:49 eat - burp	20:44 answer her	21:41 nod your head
19:04 tips her	19:50 tables	20:45 news reel	21:42 on a train
19:05 topsoil	19:51 tablet	20:46 nicer age	21:43 new drum
19:06 tips a witch	20:01 honey is sweet	20:47 Noah's ark	21:44 underwear
19:07 toupee is wig	20:02 nice son	20:48 nice roof	21:45 new trial
19:08 tipsy wife	20:03 knows his math	20:49 nice robe	21:46 no trash
19:09 hit the busboy	20:04 necessary	21:01 window seat	22:01 Nuns eat
19:10 diabetes	20:05 nice sale	21:02 end zone	22:02 no, no son
19:11 hot potato	20:06 nice switch	21:03 handsome	22:03 in a nice home
19:12 deep down	20:07 niece is weak	21:04 needs her	22:04 Nuns hair
19:13 top team	20:08 nice sofa	21:05 window sill	22:05 no nozzle
19:14 tap water	20:09 noisy subway	21:06 window sash	22:06 own a nice watch
19:15 top hotel	20:10 nice days	21:07 new desk	22:07 Nun is awake
19:16 top dish	20:11 nice Dad	21:08 need a sofa	22:08 Nun is heavy
19:17 tape deck	20:12 nice tan	21:09 hand soap	22:09 onion soup
19:18 deep dive	20:13 nice time	21:10 haunted house	22:10 no windows
19:19 tip top	20:14 insider	21:11 knitted hat	22:11 in and out
19:20 head pains	20:15 nice deal	21:12 hunt down	22:12 no antenna
19:21 deep end	20:16 nice touch	21:13 night time	22:13 on a new time
19:22 eat banana	20:17 nest egg	21:14 anteater	22:14 non odor
19:23 top name	20:18 nose dive	21:15 need a hotel	22:15 no night owl
19:24 top owner	20:19 instep	21:16 need a dish	22:16 onion dish
19:25 wet pinwheel	20:20 nuisance	21:17 hound dog	22:17 no, no doggy
19:26 hit - punch	20:21 nice window	21:18 nodded off	22:18 on and off
19:27 tipping	20:22 on CNN	21:19 knotted up	22:19 onion dip
19:28 tip knife	20:23 nice name	21:20 Indians	22:20 no onions
19:29 top knob	20:24 nice honor	21:21 night, night	22:21 no one knew it
19:30 wet palms	20:25 knees kneel	21:22 Indiana won	22:22 no, no, no, no

22:23 no one knew him	22:69 union job	23:44 on my rear	24:34 no rumor
22:24 non owner	22:70 winnings	23:45 no moral	24:35 normal
22:25 onion on the hill	22:71 union coat	23:46 in my reach	24:36 narrow match
22:26 in a nice niche	23:01 no mist	23:47 in America	24:37 newer mug
22:27 no yawning	23:02 no my son	23:48 on my roof	24:38 newer movie
22:28 own a new knife	23:03 new museum	23:49 on my robe	24:39 on ramp
22:29 onion knob	23:04 no miser	23:50 animals	24:40 no errors
22:30 no names	23:05 no missile	23:51 in my wallet	24:41 narrow road
22:31 no one hummed	23:06 name switch	23:52 enemy line	24:42 Henry Aaron
22:32 union man	23:07 no mask	23:53 unmail them	24:43 honorarium
22:33 no no Mom	23:08 in my safe	23:54 name a lawyer	24:44 on your rear
22:34 union hammer	23:09 no mess up	23:55 namely all	24:45 honor roll
22:35 any new mail	23:10 unmade house	23:56 on my eyelash	24:46 honor the rich
22:36 onion match	23:11 name date	24:01 unrest	24:47 honor your guy
22:37 union mug	23:12 new mitten	24:02 in Arizona	24:48 on our roof
22:38 neon movie	23:13 new medium	24:03 honors me	24:49 honor Rabbi
22:39 union map	23:14 new motor	24:04 nursery	24:50 win or lose
22:40 win honors	23:15 no medal	24:05 no resale	24:51 new world
22:41 non road	23:16 enemy dish	24:06 owners wish	24:52 narrow lawn
22:42 the union ran	23:17 own my dog	24:07 no rescue	24:53 no realm
22:43 Union Army	23:18 own my TV	24:08 New Year's Eve	24:54 new ruler
22:44 neon rear	23:19 in my tub	24:09 newer soap	24:55 near oil well
22:45 union railway	23:20 no mayonnaise	24:10 no radios	24:56 newer leash
22:46 in any rush	23:21 in my window	24:11 honor the dead	24:57 on your leg
22:47 in New York	23:22 in my union	24:12 no radio on	24:58 win her love
22:48 neon roof	23:23 in my name	24:13 on your dime	24:59 on your lip
22:49 union rope	23:24 in my honor	24:14 no radar	24:60 no riches
22:50 no nails	23:25 name on wall	24:15 on your dial	24:61 unreached
22:51 neon light	23:26 on my nacho	24:16 newer dish	24:62 Norwegian
22:52 new nylon	23:27 numbing	24:17 narrow deck	24:63 newer gym
22:53 on any limb	23:28 on my knife	24:18 unheard of	24:64 no richer
22:54 onion layer	23:29 new man I hope	24:19 on your top	24:65 New Rochelle
22:55 own an oil well	23:30 in my maze	24:20 no runs	24:66 honor Judge
22:56 neon leash	23:31 now I'm mad	24:21 no rent	24:67 no rich guy
22:57 neon leg	23:32 win my man	24:22 no reunion	25:01 win lawsuit
22:58 neon leaf	23:33 know my Mom	24:23 own your name	25:02 kneel son
22:59 neon lip	23:34 no memory	24:24 no rain here	25:03 nails them
22:60 no nachos	23:35 in my mail	24:25 no rain, hail	25:04 new laser
22:61 on a new sheet	23:36 won my match	24:26 on the range	25:05 nails wall
22:62 own a nation	23:37 on my mug	24:27 honoring	25:06 nail switch
22:63 neon gym	23:38 in my movie	24:28 no runoff	25:07 nails wig
22:64 in a new chair	23:39 enemy map	24:29 no run up	25:08 kneels off
22:65 neon jail	23:40 no more ice	24:30 enormous	25:09 nails up
22:66 neon Judge	23:41 win my heart	24:31 in warm heat	25:10 no lettuce
22:67 Union Jack	23:42 no more honey	24:32 win your man	25:11 annihilated
22:68 non chef	23:43 in my room	24:33 honor Mom	25:12 nail down

25:13 annihilate them	26:05 new chisel	26:51 unshelled	27:22 hang on now
25:14 annihilator	26:06 when she's shy	26:52 one huge loan	27:23 nickname
25:15 no ladle	26:07 nachos - OK	26:53 in chilly home	27:24 weighing on her
25:16 nailed shoe	26:08 enjoys the eve	26:54 no chili here	27:25 in the canal
25:17 an old guy	26:09 inches up	26:55 on huge oil well	27:26 new gun show
25:18 newlywed wife	26:10 no shots	26:56 on a huge leash	27:27 honking
25:19 no let up	26:11 when she died	26:57 no jelly, OK	27:28 yank on/off
25:20 nylon hose	26:12 new showtune	26:58 unshelf	27:29 young'in boy
25:21 no land	26:13 new show time	26:59 no jelly pie	27:30 win games
25:22 new linen	26:14 no chowder	26:60 enjoy shows	27:31 weighing meat
25:23 only a name	26:15 new huge toll	26:61 new huge jet	27:32 young man
25:24 nylon wire	26:16 new huge dish	26:62 no shoe shine	27:33 weighing Mom
25:25 noel, noel	26:17 new show dog	26:63 in a huge gym	27:34 weighing more
25:26 no lunch	26:18 no shut off	26:64 in huge shower	27:35 weighing mail
25:27 nailing	26:19 now shut up	26:65 in a huge jail	27:36 weighing much
25:28 nylon half	26:20 nations	26:66 a hunch Judge	27:37 yank hammock
25:29 no line-up	26:21 nationwide	26:67 one huge shake	27:38 knock him off
25:30 no limbs	26:22 now shine on	26:68 on edge chef	27:39 knock him up
25:31 nail mat	26:23 now join me	26:69 one huge ship	27:40 new cars
25:32 only money	26:24 engineer	26:70 when she goes	27:41 new grad
25:33 only Mom	26:25 national	26:71 no jacket	27:42 unicorn
25:34 nail hammer	26:26 no change	26:72 no shakin'	27:43 anagram
25:35 only a male	26:27 no junk	26:73 one huge comb	27:44 new career
25:36 only my wish	26:28 new huge knife	26:74 no joker	27:45 uncurl
25:37 only a mug	26:29 enjoy a nap	26:75 unshackle	27:46 Anchorage
25:38 only a movie	26:30 new chums	27:01 no guest	27:47 new crack
25:39 in limbo	26:31 unjammed	27:02 Yankees win	27:48 engrave
25:40 no yellow rose	26:32 enjoy money	27:03 wings me away	27:49 neck rub
25:41 on alert	26:33 enjoy Miami	27:04 Yankees hour	27:50 wine glass
25:42 only rain	26:34 enjoy more	27:05 in a castle	27:51 include
25:43 in yellow room	26:35 enjoy the meal	27:06 new quiz show	27:52 unclean
25:44 kneel - roar	26:36 enjoy match	27:07 yanks wig	27:53 unclaim
25:45 kneel - roll	26:37 enjoy my walk	27:08 knocks off	27:54 unclear
25:46 enlarge	26:38 enjoy movie	27:09 wings up	27:55 an ugly whale
25:47 nail rug	26:39 no shampoo	27:10 neckties	27:56 English
25:48 nail roof	26:40 New Jersey	27:11 uncoated	27:57 an ugly guy
25:49 only a robe	26:41 injured	27:12 knockdown	27:58 no glove
25:51 only a wallet	26:42 on a journey	27:13 Yankee team	27:59 unclip
25:52 only a loan	26:43 inchworm	27:14 knock door	27:60 engages
25:53 only lamb	26:44 no chair here	27:15 in kettle	27:61 ink jet
25:54 only a lawyer	26:45 on a huge rail	27:16 Yankee Dutch	27:62 win, coach, win
25:55 only a lily	26:46 in church	27:17 naked guy	27:63 young chum
26:01 unjust	26:47 knee jerk	27:18 knock it off	27:64 hung jury
26:02 unchosen	26:48 no sheriff	27:19 hang it up	27:65 yank the shell
26:03 nachos - yum!	26:49 no cherry pie	27:20 nick nose	27:66 young Judge
26:04 enjoys war	26:50 no jails	27:21 knock on wood	28:01 invest

28:02 naive son	28:48 on heavy roof	29:26 Hawaiian Punch	30:26 I'm a snitch
28:03 envies them	28:49 Navy rope	29:27 new bank	30:27 missing
28:04 no officer	28:50 no flies	29:28 unhappy, naive	30:28 messy knife
28:05 Navy Seal	28:51 inflate	29:29 nap, nap	30:29 messin' up
28:06 on/off switch	28:52 win a violin	29:30 no bombs	30:30 museums
28:07 envies the guy	28:53 no volume	29:31 unhappy maid	30:31 mass media
28:08 new face-off	28:54 no valor	29:32 unhappy man	30:32 messy man
28:09 now face up	28:55 NFL law	29:33 unhappy Mom	30:33 I miss Mom
28:10 new videos	28:56 no flesh	29:34 unhappy Mayor	30:34 messy Mayor
28:11 invaded	28:57 no flack	29:35 unhappy male	30:35 miss a meal
28:12 invite in	28:58 no fluff	29:36 unhappy match	30:36 mismatch
28:13 invade them	28:59 envelope	29:37 nap - hammock	30:37 may I smoke
28:14 no food here	28:60 no fishes	29:38 unhappy movie	30:38 museum fee
28:15 knife dull	28:61 unfished	29:39 no bump	30:39 I'm so mopey
28:16 new food show	28:62 no ovation	29:40 neighbors	30:40 miseries
28:17 invade the guy	28:63 Navaho chum	29:41 neighborhood	30:41 misread
28:18 unfit wife	28:64 in heavy chair	29:42 NBA arena	30:42 miss the rain
28:19 navy top	28:65 unofficial	29:43 own a broom	30:43 messy room
28:20 no finesse	28:66 naive judge	29:44 no barrier	31:01 midwest
28:21 invent	28:67 Navaho Chief	29:45 neighborly	31:02 medicine
28:22 unfunny hen	28:68 knife - chef	29:46 no brush	31:03 meets him
28:23 uneven hem	29:01 no pest	30:01 misused	31:04 meets her
28:24 uneven hair	29:02 no poison	30:02 Miss USA won	31:05 muddy soil
28:25 no vinyl	29:03 no buys, hmm	30:03 misses him	31:06 made switch
28:26 unfinish	29:04 unbusy hour	30:04 I'm so sorry	31:07 I'm too sick
28:27 knifing	29:05 new puzzle	30:05 misses a wheel	31:08 met his wife
28:28 on/off, on/off	29:06 new passage	30:06 misses a shoe	31:09 muddy soup
28:29 now phone up	29:07 knapsack	30:07 I'm so sick	31:10 muddy toes
28:30 infamous	29:08 now pass off	30:08 I'm so safe	31:11 meditate
28:31 knife the meat	29:09 no pass up	30:09 Mississippi	31:12 midtown
28:32 Navaho woman	29:10 no pets	30:10 moist eyes	31:13 made it home
28:33 a Navy Mom	29:11 unpadded	30:11 misty eyed	31:14 matador
28:34 Navy hammer	29:12 unbutton	30:12 messy den	31:15 made it well
28:35 no heavy mail	29:13 nap time	30:13 home sweet home	31:16 mad dash
28:36 Navaho match	29:14 no butter	30:14 hamster	31:17 mad dog
28:37 Navy mug	29:15 wine bottle	30:15 misdial	31:18 mute TV
28:38 Navy movie	29:16 unpaid wage	30:16 mustache	31:19 made it up
28:39 Navy map	29:17 nip/tuck	30:17 mystic	31:20 mittens
28:40 universe	29:18 now pay it off	30:18 my staff	31:21 midnight
28:41 on Friday	29:19 now pay it up	30:19 messed up	31:22 mitten on
28:42 no frown	29:20 no pens	30:20 messy nose	31:23 made a name
28:43 uniform	29:21 one pint	30:21 Amazon heat	31:24 hometown hero
28:44 no fire here	29:22 no opinion	30:22 messy nun	31:25 my toenail
28:45 unfurl	29:23 unhappy gnome	30:23 missin' him	31:26 muddy nacho
28:46 unfresh	29:24 wine opener	30:24 missin' her	31:27 mating
28:47 no frog	29:25 on a bony heel	30:25 I'm senile	31:28 muddy knife

31:29 mitten boy	32:20 mean, nosy	33:14 Mommy dear	34:04 my rosy hair
31:30 Mighty Mouse	32:21 money hound	33:15 my motel	34:05 morsel
31:31 medium height	32:22 mean Nun	33:16 Mom hid wash	34:06 marry his wish
31:32 madman	32:23 mean name	33:17 Miami dog	34:07 more sick
31:33 meet Mom	32:24 mean owner	33:18 Mom ate half	34:08 marry his wife
31:34 medium hair	32:25 women only	33:19 Mom had a boy	34:09 more soap
31:35 medium well	32:26 mini nacho	33:20 Mom knows	34:10 merits
31:36 medium age	32:27 mining	33:21 my mint	34:11 marry today
31:37 muddy mug	32:28 man 'n wife	33:22 My man won	34:12 martini
31:38 meet my wife	32:29 men nap	33:23 Mom knew him	34:13 maritime
31:39 muddy map	32:30 Minnie Mouse	33:24 Miami owner	34:14 murder
31:40 mattress	32:31 a woman I me	33:25 Mom knew all	34:15 marital
31:41 maître d	32:32 man / woman	33:26 hey Mom, enjoy	34:16 ham, radish
31:42 my train	32:33 mean mom	33:27 I'm my own guy	34:17 a married guy
31:43 humdrum	32:34 many more	33:28 mummy in half	34:18 mortify
31:44 motor here	32:35 main meal	33:29 Mom, nap	34:19 a married boy
31:45 motor oil	32:36 mean match	33:30 Mom may see you	34:20 marathons
31:46 my trash	32:37 many may walk	33:31 Mom, may I eat	34:21 marinate
31:47 Amtrak	32:38 run him off	33:32 Miami moon	34:22 my reunion
31:48 midriff	32:39 Maine map	33:33 Mommy, Mommy	34:23 more numb
31:49 home tribe	32:40 minors	33:34 Mom may hear	34:24 mariner
31:50 motels	32:41 human heart	33:35 my home meal	34:25 hammer nail
31:51 meddled	32:42 mini rain	33:36 my home match	34:26 maroon shoe
31:52 medallion	32:43 run her home	33:37 Mom, may I go	34:27 hammering
31:53 Ma, tell me	32:44 I'm in error	33:38 Mom, move	34:28 hammer / knife
31:54 I'm taller	32:45 monorail	33:39 Miami map	34:29 may I run by
31:55 metal wheel	32:46 money rich	33:40 memories	34:30 homerooms
32:01 Minnesota	32:47 monarch	33:41 Mom read	34:31 mermaid
32:02 monsoon	32:48 mean / rough	33:42 my homerun	34:32 Mormon
32:03 mini swim	32:49 minor boy	33:43 Miami room	34:33 me or Mom
32:04 menswear	32:50 manuals	33:44 my mirror	34:34 murmur
32:05 mean seal	32:51 moon light	33:45 memorial	34:35 more mail
32:06 men's watch	32:52 mean lion	33:46 memory wish	34:36 more mush
32:07 women's wig	33:01 Miami's hot	33:47 memory weak	34:37 marry me, OK
32:08 man's wife	33:02 Mom's a honey	33:48 Miami rough	35:01 I'm lost
32:09 minesweep	33:03 Mom's home	33:49 hem may rip	35:02 I'm loose now
32:10 mints	33:04 Mom's here	33:50 mammals	35:03 mauls him
32:11 mandate	33:05 Mom's well	33:51 Mom will eat	35:04 mail is here
32:12 mountain	33:06 Moms age	33:52 my melon	35:05 meal is well
32:13 menu item	33:07 Mom's weak	33:53 Mom will hum	35:06 meal is chewy
32:14 monitor	33:08 Mom is a wife	33:54 Miami lawyer	35:07 meal is OK
32:15 mantel	33:09 Mama's boy	33:55 Mom will yell	35:08 mail is off
32:16 main dish	33:10 my mates	33:56 Mom will age	35:09 mail swap
32:17 mean dog	33:11 I'm mad at you	34:01 Mayor's aide	35:10 melodies
32:18 minute off	33:12 my hometown	34:02 I'm your son	35:11 melted
32:19 Manitoba	33:13 Mom ate ham	34:03 hammers me	35:12 mail it in

35:13 melt me	36:24 machinery	37:27 mechanic	38:33 move Mom
35:14 mild weather	36:25 emotional	37:28 magnify	38:34 move my hair
35:15 melt hill	36:26 my change	37:29 makin' whoopie	38:35 move the mail
35:16 melt shoe	36:27 matching	37:30 make a mess	38:36 move the match
35:17 mile to go	36:28 my huge knife	37:31 make my day	38:37 move my wig
35:18 mild wave	36:29 machine boy	37:32 make money	38:38 move him off
35:19 I'm laid up	36:30 mash thumbs	37:33 mug Mom	38:39 move me up
35:20 melons	36:31 much meat	37:34 my camera	38:40 home fries
35:21 melon head	36:32 much money	37:35 my camel	38:41 I'm fired
35:22 I'm alone now	36:33 mash my thumb	37:36 make me age	39:01 I'm a pest
35:23 melon / ham	36:34 match my hair	37:37 make me go	39:02 I'm busy now
35:24 millionaire	36:35 much mail	37:38 make a move	39:03 mops the home
35:25 I'm lonely	36:36 match my shoe	37:39 home camp	39:04 I'm busier
35:26 melon wash	36:37 match my wig	37:40 I'm crazy	39:05 maybe a sale
35:27 mailing	36:38 match my half	38:01 I'm fast	39:06 maybe a switch
35:28 melon half	36:39 my shampoo	38:02 move son	39:07 I'm a busy guy
35:29 melon pie	36:40 measures	38:03 moves home	39:08 I'm a busy wife
35:30 I'm all messy	36:41 measured	38:04 move sir	39:09 maybe soup
35:31 malamute	36:42 my journey	38:05 moves wall	39:10 empty house
35:32 mailman	36:43 mushroom	38:06 he moves watch	39:11 emptied
35:33 mail my ham	37:01 my guest	38:07 movie is OK	39:12 empty wine
35:34 a mile more	37:02 magazine	38:08 move is off	39:13 empty home
35:35 mail my will	37:03 makes a home	38:09 moves up	39:14 I'm better
36:01 majesty	37:04 makes war	38:10 my videos	39:15 embattle
36:02 match is on	37:05 my castle	38:11 I'm faded	39:16 empty shoe
36:03 matches him	37:06 makes a show	38:12 move it now	39:17 mop deck
36:04 matches her	37:07 Mexico	38:13 move it home	39:18 I'm paid off
36:05 my chisel	37:08 makes off	38:14 move the door	39:19 I'm paid up
36:06 matches shoe	37:09 makes up	38:15 movie deal	39:20 my bonus
36:07 match sock	37:10 maggots	38:16 move dish	39:21 home bound
36:08 match is off	37:11 I'm a cadet	38:17 move dog	39:22 Yum! banana
36:09 match is up	37:12 my kitten	38:18 move the TV	39:23 mop in home
36:10 matched his	37:13 make it home	38:19 I'm fed up	39:24 I'm a pioneer
36:11 I'm shut out	37:14 my guitar	38:20 muffins	39:25 map on wall
36:12 I'm shut in	37:15 make it well	38:21 move on it	39:26 homey bunch
36:13 match dime	37:16 make it chewy	38:22 move onion	39:27 mopping
36:14 my shutter	37:17 make it walk	38:23 move on home	39:28 maybe the Navy
36:15 my huge deal	37:18 make it wave	38:24 move in here	39:29 my pin up
36:16 mash dish	37:19 make it up	38:25 my final	39:30 my poems
36:17 my huge deck	37:20 my guns	38:26 my funny shoe	39:31 I'm bombed
36:18 much TV	37:21 magnet	38:27 moving	39:32 map man
36:19 match it up	37:22 mug a Nun	38:28 muffin heavy	39:33 maybe Mom
36:20 machines	37:23 magnum	38:29 move on up	39:34 maybe more
36:21 my chant	37:24 mug the owner	38:30 move my house	39:35 mopey male
36:22 may I join in	37:25 make a nail	38:31 move my head	39:36 mopey match
36:23 match name	37:26 I'm gun shy	38:32 move my wine	39:37 maybe I'm ok

39:38 maybe movie	40:41 resort	41:38 write him off	42:27 running
39:39 maybe, maybe	40:42 Rice a roni	41:39 road map	42:28 reunion off
39:40 umpires	40:43 rosy room	41:40 writers	42:29 run - nap
39:41 import	40:44 raise her hair	41:41 red heart	42:30 ruin my house
39:42 I'm a Brownie	40:45 ears hear well	41:42 return	42:31 run him out
39:43 my broom	40:46 research	41:43 redo room	42:32 rainman
40:01 resist	40:47 rosy rug	41:44 road warrior	42:33 run Mom
40:02 raise a son	40:48 raise the roof	41:45 rod / reel	42:34 rain more
40:03 racism	40:49 our syrup	41:46 road rage	42:35 run mail
40:04 rice, sir	41:01 right side	41:47 our truck	42:36 run the match
40:05 hears so well	41:02 redesign	41:48 rude, rough	42:37 ruin my walk
40:06 raise switch	41:03 writes home	41:49 ear drop	42:38 run him off
40:07 you're so sick	41:04 writes her	41:50 rattles	43:01 you're misty
40:08 race is off	41:05 yard sale	41:51 retaliate	43:02 hire me soon
40:09 raises up	41:06 yard is huge	41:52 ride alone	43:03 hair museum
40:10 rest easy	41:07 red sock	41:53 redial him	43:04 room is airy
40:11 rusted	41:08 radio is off	41:54 retailer	43:05 arm is well
40:12 rest in	41:09 ride the subway	41:55 red lily	43:06 hour massage
40:13 rest home	41:10 rodeo days	41:56 red leash	43:07 hear the music
40:14 rooster	41:11 red toad	41:57 right leg	43:08 room safe
40:15 hair style	41:12 red town	42:01 runs out	43:09 arms up
40:16 wrist watch	41:13 right time	42:02 runs in	43:10 remedies
40:17 we're stuck	41:14 red door	42:03 ransom	43:11 hear my Dad
40:18 raise the TV	41:15 radio dial	42:04 rinse hair	43:12 warm tuna
40:19 rest up	41:16 red dish	42:05 rinse well	43:13 warm dime
40:20 raisins	41:17 heart attack	42:06 runs wash	43:14 warm water
40:21 Arizona heat	41:18 radio / TV	42:07 ransack	43:15 armadillo
40:22 resign now	41:19 road top	42:08 rinse off	43:16 armed shoe
40:23 reassign me	41:20 red nose	42:09 runs by	43:17 arithmetic
40:24 Arizona air	41:21 right hand	42:10 warrants	43:18 hear my TV
40:25 raisin hill	41:22 red onion	42:11 rented	43:19 you're my type
40:26 you're a snitch	41:23 write name	42:12 run down	43:20 romance
40:27 rising	41:24 award winner	42:13 random	43:21 warm window
40:28 raise a knife	41:25 through tunnel	42:14 reindeer	43:22 hear my union
40:29 raisin pie	41:26 rotten shoe	42:15 rental	43:23 hear my name
40:30 resumes	41:27 writing	42:16 round shoe	43:24 roman war
40:31 raise my head	41:28 written off	42:17 run, eat, walk	43:25 Roman wall
40:32 raise money	41:29 radio knob	42:18 round off	43:26 warm nacho
40:33 rosy Mom	41:30 your dimes	42:19 round up	43:27 harmonica
40:34 raise hammer	41:31 red meat	42:20 runny nose	43:28 Army - Navy
40:35 you're smelly	41:32 write him in	42:21 rainy night	43:29 roman pie
40:36 raise my shoe	41:33 write Mom	42:22 reunion on	43:30 room messy
40:37 you're smoky	41:34 here tomorrow	42:23 rain on me	43:31 roommate
40:38 rosy movie	41:35 read mail	42:24 rain on her	43:32 Army man
40:39 raise me up	41:36 right match	42:25 rain on all	43:33 hear my Mom
40:40 razors	41:37 radio mic	42:26 rain on shoe	43:34 weary memory

44:01 rear seat	45:13 real dumb	46:31 rich maid	48:12 rough town
44:02 her reason	45:14 realtor	46:32 rich man	48:13 rough time
44:03 roars home	45:15 worldly	46:33 rich Mom	48:14 rough water
44:04 her razor	45:16 real touchy	46:34 Rushmore	48:15 rough hotel
44:05 rehearsal	45:17 real dog	47:01 request	48:16 refit shoe
44:06 rewire switch	45:18 world view	47:02 rakes in	48:17 rough dog
44:07 air rescue	45:19 roll the tape	47:03 wrecks home	48:18 rough TV
44:08 rear is off	45:20 hair lines	47:04 wrecks hair	48:19 roof top
44:09 rears up	45:21 real neat	47:05 rakes well	48:20 ravens
44:10 your rights	45:22 a real Nun	47:06 rugs wash	48:21 refund
44:11 rewrite it	45:23 real name	47:07 rookies walk	48:22 rough Nun
44:12 your radio on	45:24 row the liner	47:08 rocks heavy	48:23 rough name
44:13 you're right Ma	45:25 you're lonely	47:09 racks up	48:24 refinery
44:14 rear door	45:26 our lunch	47:10 rockets	48:25 roof nail
44:15 your rattle	45:27 reeling	47:11 wear coat / tie	48:26 orphanage
44:16 our radish	45:28 real naive	47:12 rag town	48:27 roofing
44:17 rear deck	46:01 hairy chest	47:13 rag time	48:28 rough knife
44:18 hear your TV	46:02 reach the sun	47:14 rocketeer	48:29 rough nap
44:19 your radio up	46:03 reaches me	47:15 rocket oil	48:30 we're famous
44:20 reruns	46:04 reaches her	47:16 rocket watch	48:31 rough meat
44:21 rear window	46:05 reaches all	47:17 raggy dog	48:32 rough woman
44:22 a rerun on	46:06 reach switch	47:18 rock TV	48:33 rough Mom
44:23 hear her name	46:07 reaches egg	47:19 rocket up	48:34 rough mare
44:24 hear a runner	46:08 your age is off	47:20 raccoons	48:35 rough meal
44:25 here or in hell	46:09 reaches up	47:21 recount	48:36 rough match
44:26 their ranch	46:10 reach toes	47:22 Reagan won	48:37 rough mug
44:27 roaring	46:11 rich Dad	47:23 raccoon home	48:38 review movie
44:28 hear the runoff	46:12 reached in	47:24 rookie owner	48:39 revamp
44:29 rear knob	46:13 reached him	47:25 Erie Canal	48:40 rivers
44:30 war rooms	46:14 reach door	47:26 hurricane watch	48:41 Harvard
44:31 rare meat	46:15 roach hotel	47:27 rocking	48:42 refrain
44:32 rare money	46:16 arched shoe	47:28 rock the Navy	48:43 reform
44:33 our hero Mom	46:17 rich Doc	47:29 year gone by	48:44 rough roar
44:34 our rumor	46:18 reach the TV	47:30 a year comes	48:45 you're frail
45:01 really sweet	46:19 reached up	47:31 hair - comb it	48:46 you're fresh
45:02 real sunny	46:20 Russians	48:01 revisit	48:47 riverwalk
45:03 roll, swim	46:21 rich aunt	48:02 refasten	49:01 rhapsody
45:04 real sore	46:22 rich Nun	48:03 rough sum	49:02 rubs in
45:05 really silly	46:23 arch enemy	48:04 hear the officer	49:03 rips me
45:06 rail switch	46:24 rich owner	48:05 refusal	49:04 rubs her
45:07 really sick	46:25 rational	48:06 rough switch	49:05 wraps well
45:08 real safe	46:26 your chance	48:07 roof is OK	49:06 rubs watch
45:09 rolls up	46:27 reaching	48:08 reviews wave	49:07 rubs wig
45:10 relates	46:28 arch knife	48:09 revs up	49:08 rubs off
45:11 related	46:29 rush on up	48:10 rivets	49:09 rips up
45:12 roll down	46:30 reach mouse	48:11 riveted	49:10 rabbits

64

49:11 riptide	50:18 lost wife	51:43 lit room	52:25 line new wall
49:12 rebutton	50:19 lost hope	51:44 yellow terrier	52:26 linen wash
49:13 rubbed him	50:20 loosens	51:45 light rail	52:27 leaning
49:14 rubbed her	50:21 loosen tie	51:46 yellow trash	52:28 linen off
49:15 reptile	51:01 lights out	51:47 yellow truck	52:29 lion nap
49:16 robbed watch	51:02 yield sign	51:48 low driveway	52:30 lion / mouse
49:17 robotic	51:03 leads him	51:49 ladder up	52:31 lean meat
49:18 rubbed off	51:04 leads her	51:50 ladles	52:32 loan money
49:19 wrapped up	51:05 let's yell	51:51 yell outloud	52:33 lion mama
49:20 ribbons	51:06 light switch	51:52 loud lion	52:34 lawn mower
49:21 Robin Hood	51:07 yellow desk	51:53 little home	53:01 lime soda
49:22 wrap onion	51:08 leads off	51:54 little hair	53:02 limousine
49:23 rob enemy	51:09 lights up	51:55 little hill	53:03 Law museum
49:24 hire pioneer	51:10 lightweights	51:56 little shoe	53:04 lime sour
49:25 harpoon whale	51:11 latitude	51:57 lady luck	53:05 lamb's wool
49:26 re-punish	51:12 lot to win	51:58 wildlife	53:06 oily massage
49:27 wrapping	51:13 lead it home	51:59 little boy	53:07 lime is OK
49:28 wrap knife	51:14 light tower	51:60 yellow dishes	53:08 limb is off
49:29 ribbon boy	51:15 loud hotel	51:61 loud jet	53:09 limb is up
49:30 wire bombs	51:16 loaded wash	51:62 Yale tuition	53:10 limits
49:31 wrap meat	51:17 old dog	51:63 old gym	53:11 limited
49:32 wrap money	51:18 loud TV	51:64 loud cheer	53:12 yellow mitten
49:33 rob Mom	51:19 loaded up	52:01 lines out	54:01 leather seat
49:34 rob hammer	51:20 loud noise	52:02 leans in	54:02 lawyers win
49:35 wrap meal	51:21 late night	52:03 lonesome	54:03 lures me
49:36 ruin my shoe	51:22 loud Nun	52:04 lancer	54:04 lowers hair
49:37 rip hammock	51:23 old name	52:05 hollow nozzle	54:05 lower sail
49:38 rip movie	51:24 loud owner	52:06 lane switch	54:06 lowers age
49:39 air pump	51:25 hollow tunnel	52:07 lion is weak	54:07 yell rescue
50:01 loses head	51:26 old niche	52:08 leans off	54:08 lowers ivy
50:02 lose sun	51:27 oil tank	52:09 lines up	54:09 lower subway
50:03 lose sum	51:28 light knife	52:10 walnuts	54:10 lords
50:04 loses hair	51:29 light nap	52:11 landed	54:11 alerted
50:05 loose soil	51:30 loud mouse	52:12 London	54:12 lower down
50:06 loses shoe	51:31 ultimate	52:13 alone at home	54:13 alert him
50:07 loses wig	51:32 old man	52:14 laundry	54:14 oily radar
50:08 yells safe	51:33 loud Mom	52:15 lion tail	54:15 yellow rattle
50:09 loses hope	51:34 loud hammer	52:16 lion dish	54:16 lower dish
50:10 lazy days	51:35 light meal	52:17 lion attack	54:17 lower deck
50:11 lazy Dad	51:36 light match	52:18 alone with TV	55:01 all lost
50:12 Yellowstone	51:37 old mug	52:19 line it up	55:02 law lesson
50:13 low sodium	51:38 Hollywood movie	52:20 linens	55:03 we'll lose him
50:14 wool sweater	51:39 old map	52:21 Halloween night	55:04 loyal Czar
50:15 last will	51:40 willow trees	52:22 the lone nun	55:05 hole, lose wheel
50:16 lost shoe	51:41 loud radio	52:23 the lone enemy	55:06 loyal switch
50:17 elastic	51:42 loud rain	52:24 a lone owner	55:07 lily is weak

55:08 oil well is heavy	57:18 all get off	60:09 chooses up	63:10 jam dose
55:09 oil well is up	57:19 hello / goodbye	60:10 justice	63:11 jammed toe
55:10 yellow wallets	57:20 look nice	60:11 watch us Dad	63:12 huge mitten
55:11 lay low today	57:21 leaky window	60:12 chase down	63:13 wash medium
55:12 oil Aladdin	58:01 love seat	60:13 just me	63:14 jam door
55:13 oily, oily dime	58:02 loves on	60:14 jester	63:15 she may tell
55:14 yellow ladder	58:03 loves me	60:15 chase tail	63:16 she may teach
55:15 well hello Dolly	58:04 loves her	60:16 washes dish	63:17 jammed key
55:16 loyal dish	58:05 loves all	60:17 chase dog	63:18 show me a TV
55:17 loyal dog	58:06 leaves a shoe	60:18 watches TV	63:19 jammed up
55:18 all let off	58:07 lovesick	60:19 juice it up	64:01 shower is hot
55:19 we'll let up	58:08 loves wife	60:20 show signs	64:02 shower is on
55:20 yellow lines	58:09 loves up	60:21 washes window	64:03 showers home
55:21 holy land	58:10 left house	60:22 chosen one	64:04 shower is here
55:22 yellow linen	58:11 loved it	61:01 huge test	64:05 juries lie
55:23 yell, yell name	58:12 leave town	61:02 jets in	64:06 cherries age
56:01 lashes out	58:13 we'll feed him	61:03 jets home	64:07 huge rescue
56:02 latches on	58:14 elevator	61:04 shoots / war	64:08 shower is off
56:03 lashes him	59:01 leaps ahead	61:05 shot a seal	64:09 shores up
56:04 leashes her	59:02 I'll buy soon	61:06 shoot, swish	64:10 shirts
56:05 I'll chisel	59:03 I'll buy some	61:07 jet ski	64:11 shirt / tie
56:06 lashes wash	59:04 I'll pass her	61:08 jets off	64:12 shorten
56:07 lashes wig	59:05 whole puzzle	61:09 shoots up	65:01 wish list
56:08 eyelashes off	59:06 lips age	61:10 she dates	65:02 chill is on
56:09 whale shows up	59:07 we'll bask	61:11 she dieted	65:03 jails him
56:10 yellow jets	59:08 I'll pass off	62:01 Ash Wednesday	65:04 chills her
56:11 lashed out	59:09 hail busboy	62:02 shines on	65:05 chilly seal
56:12 latched on	59:10 yellow beads	62:03 chains him	65:06 chili is chewy
56:13 latch the dome	59:11 oily potato	62:04 Chinese year	65:07 huge - Alaska
57:01 he likes it	59:12 yellow button	62:05 Chinese wall	65:08 chill is off
57:02 logs on	59:13 well bottom	62:06 Chinese shoe	65:09 chili soup
57:03 locksmith	59:14 yellow butter	62:07 Chinese guy	65:10 shields
57:04 I like his hair	59:15 we'll battle	62:08 Chinese wife	65:11 childhood
57:05 look silly	59:16 I'll buy dish	62:09 shines up	65:12 child won
57:06 likes the watch	59:17 lap to go	62:10 chants	65:13 jail time
57:07 look sick	59:18 leaped off	62:11 chanted	65:14 shoulder
57:08 lock safe	59:19 lap top	62:12 Chinatown	65:15 a child will
57:09 looks up	59:20 whale bones	63:01 jams it	65:16 childish
57:10 yellow cats	60:01 chooses it	63:02 jams, honey	65:17 chili dog
57:11 leg it out	60:02 chase scene	63:03 shames me	65:18 shield off
57:12 look down	60:03 chooses me	63:04 she may swear	65:19 shield up
57:13 I liked him	60:04 chooses her	63:05 huge muzzle	65:20 show lines
57:14 alligator	60:05 chooses well	63:06 watch massage	65:21 chilly night
57:15 I liked L.A.	60:06 shows his watch	63:07 huge mask	65:22 huge linen
57:16 lick dish	60:07 watches us go	63:08 shame is off	63:01 jams it
57:17 locked key	60:08 chases off	63:09 jams up	63:02 jams, honey

63:03 shames me	65:18 shield off	68:08 shaves off	69:19 chip tub
63:04 Jim is here	65:19 shield up	68:09 shoves by	69:20 Japanese
63:05 huge muzzle	65:20 show lines	68:10 show videos	69:21 job hunt
63:06 watch massage	65:21 chilly night	68:11 shifted	69:22 chop onion
63:07 huge mask	65:22 huge linen	68:12 chieftain	69:23 jab enemy
63:08 shame is off	65:23 chill on him	68:13 shoved him	69:24 wash pioneer
63:09 jams up	65:24 huge liner	68:14 shaved hair	69:25 chop only
63:10 shammed us	65:25 shy, lonely	68:15 chew off tail	69:26 huge punch
63:11 jammed toe	66:01 judges it	68:16 shove dish	69:27 shopping
63:12 huge mitten	66:02 judge is in	68:17 shave dog	69:28 chip knife
63:13 jammed thumb	66:03 judges me	68:18 shaved off	69:29 choppy nap
63:14 jam door	66:04 judges her	68:19 shave top	69:30 huge bombs
63:15 she may tell	66:05 judges well	68:20 huge phones	69:31 chop meat
63:16 she may teach	66:06 judges show	68:21 edge of night	69:32 cheap man
63:17 jammed key	66:07 judge is weak	68:22 shave a Nun	69:33 shop Mom
63:18 show me TV	66:08 judge is heavy	68:23 shove enemy	69:34 shop more
63:19 jammed up	66:09 judges boy	68:24 shove owner	69:35 shop - mall
64:01 shower is hot	66:10 judged us	68:25 watch the final	69:36 job match
64:02 shower is on	66:11 judged it	68:26 show finish	70:01 exhaust
64:03 showers home	66:12 huge show tune	68:27 shaving	70:02 cases won
64:04 shower is here	66:13 judged him	68:28 shove knife	70:03 kisses him
64:05 juries lie	66:14 judged her	68:29 chew off knob	70:04 kisses her
64:06 cherries age	66:15 judged well	68:30 she fumes	70:05 excel
64:07 huge rescue	66:16 judged show	68:31 shave my head	71:01 good city
64:08 shower is off	66:17 judge a dog	68:32 shave a man	71:02 good son
64:09 shores up	66:18 judged wife	68:33 shave mummy	71:03 cats meow
64:10 shirts	66:19 she chewed pie	68:34 shave my hair	71:04 gets her
64:11 shirt / tie	66:20 huge chains	68:35 shove mail	71:05 waggy tassel
64:12 shorten	66:21 she joined	69:01 cheap seat	71:06 gets wish
65:01 wish list	66:22 Jewish Nun	69:02 chip in	71:07 get sick
65:02 chill is on	66:23 Jewish name	69:03 chops ham	71:08 go to sofa
65:03 jails him	66:24 judge winner	69:04 chops hair	71:09 gets up
65:04 chills her	67:01 checks out	69:05 chips wall	71:10 got dizzy
65:05 chilly seal	67:02 wage - casino	69:06 job switch	71:11 cut it out
65:06 chili is chewy	67:03 checks him	69:07 chops egg	71:12 good town
65:07 huge - Alaska	67:04 checks hair	69:08 chops off	71:13 good time
65:08 chill is off	67:05 shakes well	69:09 chops up	71:14 good tire
65:09 chili soup	67:06 checks wash	69:10 chop toes	71:15 coat tail
65:10 shields	67:07 jogs OK	69:11 chipped tooth	71:16 get a dish
65:11 childhood	68:01 chef's hat	69:12 chipped in	71:17 guide dog
65:12 a child won	68:02 chef is in	69:13 chopped ham	71:18 good TV
65:13 jail time	68:03 chef is home	69:14 chapter	71:19 good tip
65:14 shoulder	68:04 shaves hair	69:15 huge battle	71:20 kittens
65:15 a child will	68:05 huge fossil	69:16 chip dish	71:21 goodnight
65:16 childish	68:06 chef's wage	69:17 shop talk	71:22 good onion
65:17 chili dog	68:07 chef's wig	69:18 chipped off	71:23 good name

71:24 good wiener	73:26 common show	76:11 catch toad	78:25 weak vinyl
72:01 conceit	73:27 combing	76:12 cash it in	78:26 go finish
72:02 gain a son	73:28 common wife	77:01 cookie is hot	78:27 coughing
72:03 canes him	74:01 crest	77:02 hog casino	78:28 cough on wife
72:04 cancer	74:02 greasy hen	77:03 cooks ham	78:29 cough on up
72:05 counsel	74:03 greasy ham	77:04 kicks her	78:30 weak fumes
72:06 walks in shoe	74:04 grocery	77:05 cake sale	78:31 go vomit
72:07 cans egg	74:05 carousel	77:06 cookie is chewy	78:32 caveman
72:08 conceive	74:06 greasy shoe	77:07 cooks egg	78:33 cough Mom
72:09 ok on subway	74:07 crazy week	77:08 kicks off	78:34 give more
72:10 weekends	74:08 caress wife	77:09 kick is up	78:35 give mail
72:11 ignited	74:09 grows up	77:10 cactus	78:36 gave much
72:12 canteen	74:10 crates	77:11 kicked toe	78:37 coffee mug
72:13 canned ham	74:11 greeted	77:12 kicked in	78:38 gave him half
72:14 country	74:12 accordion	77:13 kicked me	78:39 coffee map
72:15 candle	74:13 greet him	77:14 kick door	78:40 givers
72:16 can't she	74:14 quarter	77:15 cocktail	78:41 go off road
72:17 Kentucky	74:15 Great Wall	77:16 cake dish	78:42 govern
72:18 hug new TV	74:16 great age	77:17 kick dog	78:43 give her ham
72:19 wagon top	74:17 critic	77:18 kicked off	78:44 gave her hair
72:20 cannons	74:18 gratify	77:19 kick it up	78:45 weak, frail
73:01 chemist	74:19 great boy	77:20 cocoons	78:46 gave her age
73:02 hug my son	74:20 cranes	78:01 OK feast	78:47 weak frog
73:03 comes home	74:21 crowned	78:02 caves in	78:48 gave her half
73:04 combs hair	74:22 corn on the ...	78:03 gives me	78:49 cover up
73:05 camisole	74:23 acronym	78:04 gives her	78:50 gavels
73:06 OK message	75:01 closet	78:05 gives all	78:51 coffee lady
73:07 combs wig	75:02 calls in	78:06 gives age	78:52 cough alone
73:08 comes off	75:03 coliseum	78:07 gave his OK	78:53 weak flame
73:09 comes up	75:04 calls her	78:08 hockey faceoff	78:54 cavalry
73:10 comedies	75:05 colossal	78:09 go fess up	78:55 give a lily
73:11 committed	75:06 glass shoe	78:10 cavities	78:56 weak flesh
73:12 comedian	75:07 classic	78:11 go feed it	78:57 UK flag
73:13 game time	75:08 closed off	78:12 caved in	78:58 week of love
73:14 combed hair	75:09 close by	78:13 go fight him	78:59 go fly up
73:15 comb tail	75:10 cleats	78:14 cafeteria	78:60 gave chase
73:16 comedy show	76:01 weak chest	78:15 gave it all	78:61 go fish day
73:17 walk my dog	76:02 cashes in	78:16 give it a wash	78:62 go fishin'
73:18 whack my TV	76:03 catches him	78:17 cough attack	78:63 go fetch him
73:19 combed up	76:04 catchers her	78:18 give it off	78:64 coffee chair
73:20 commons	76:05 catch seal	78:19 coughed up	78:65 give Jello away
73:21 community	76:06 catch show	78:20 coffins	78:66 coffee, Judge
73:22 communion	76:07 catches egg	78:21 go vent	78:67 coffee shake
73:23 hack my name	76:08 catches wave	78:22 coffee anyone	78:68 cough, shave
73:24 commoner	76:09 catches up	78:23 cough on him	78:69 gave job away
73:25 common law	76:10 coached us	78:24 cough on her	78:70 gave keys away

78:71 go fake it	81:13 feed team	85:05 falsely	88:14 half off tire
78:72 give gun away	81:14 foot odor	85:06 false wish	88:15 half off hotel
79:01 keeps it	81:15 voodoo doll	85:07 flu, sick	88:16 half off dish
79:02 keeps on	81:16 food dish	85:08 philosophy	88:17 half of deck
79:03 keeps me	82:01 have a nice day	85:09 flies up	88:18 half off TV
79:04 keeps her	82:02 funny son	85:10 flood house	89:01 heavy post
79:05 capsule	82:03 fun is home	85:11 flooded	89:02 have passion
79:06 keeps a wish	82:04 fun is here	85:12 fall down	89:03 VP is home
79:07 keepsake	82:05 heavy nozzle	85:13 follow time	89:12 heavy baton
79:08 keeps off	82:06 phone switch	86:01 half jest	89:13 off by a dime
79:09 keeps up	82:07 often sick	86:02 have chosen	89:14 FBI door
79:10 kept us	82:08 phone is off	86:03 half chase him	89:15 heavy battle
79:11 copped out	83:01 have my soda	86:04 fishes here	89:16 FBI dish
79:12 captain	83:02 famous wine	86:05 fishes well	89:17 FBI dog
79:13 keep time	83:03 famous home	86:06 fish switch	89:18 half paid off
80:01 faces it	83:04 famous hair	86:07 fudges week	89:19 half paid up
80:02 faces in	83:05 famously	86:08 fishes off	89:20 heavy pianos
80:03 faces me	83:06 have a message	86:09 fetches boy	89:21 viewpoint
80:04 faces her	83:07 famous guy	86:10 heavy jets	89:22 heavy banana
80:05 voice is well	83:08 famous wife	86:11 vegetate	89:23 VIP name
80:06 heavy seas wash	83:09 foams up	86:12 fish town	89:24 heavy pioneer
80:07 wife is sick	83:10 vomits	86:13 fudge time	89:25 off by a nil
80:08 faces off	83:11 vomited	86:14 fetch water	89:26 heavy punch
80:09 faces up	83:12 vomit honey	86:15 fetched oil	89:27 fibbing
80:10 wife sits	83:13 wife, madam	86:16 fish dish	89:28 FBI, Navy
80:11 vested	83:14 vomit here	86:17 fish dock	89:29 wife - a pin-up
80:12 feast on	83:15 heavy metal	87:01 off the coast	89:30 heavy bombs
80:13 office time	83:16 vomit hash	87:02 vaccine	89:31 VP met you
80:14 visitor	83:17 have my dog	87:03 fakes him	89:32 FBI man
80:15 half stale	83:18 have my TV	87:04 fakes her	89:33 VIP Mom
80:16 fast wash	84:01 frost	87:05 fakes all	89:34 off by more
80:17 fast guy	84:02 frozen	87:06 fakes age	89:35 FBI mail
80:18 face TV	84:03 fires me	87:07 fake sick	89:36 FBI match
80:19 fist up	84:04 freezer	88:01 have a feast	89:37 FBI mug
81:01 fades out	84:05 Ferris Wheel	88:02 heavy fasten	89:38 FBI movie
81:02 fades in	84:06 frees shoe	88:03 have wives home	89:39 heavy pump
81:03 fights me	84:07 fresco	88:04 have wives here	89:40 half price
81:04 feet sore	84:08 frees wife	88:05 half off sale	89:41 vibrate
81:05 fights well	84:09 Frisbee	88:06 half off switch	89:42 VP ran
81:06 food is chewy	84:10 overdose	88:07 half, off sack	89:43 heavy broom
81:07 food is weak	84:11 freed head	88:08 half off sofa	89:44 February
81:08 fight's off	84:12 free town	88:09 half off soap	89:45 FBI roll
81:09 fights boy	85:01 velocity	88:10 half off days	89:46 heavy brush
81:10 faded house	85:02 Phillies win	88:11 half off today	89:47 fabric
81:11 faded hat	85:03 follows me	88:12 half off tuna	89:48 FBI rough
81:12 faded in	85:04 follows her	88:13 wife fed me	89:49 FBI rope

89:50 fabulous
89:51 heavy plate
89:52 heavy plane
90:01 passes it
90:02 passes on
90:03 passes him
90:04 bosses her
90:05 passes law
90:06 buys his watch
90:07 passes egg
90:08 passes off
90:09 passes up
90:10 pests
90:11 posted
90:12 Boston
90:13 passed him
90:14 poster
90:15 postal
90:16 upstage
90:17 buys a dog
91:01 Pizza Hut
91:02 bad sun
91:03 potassium
91:04 Budweiser
91:05 beats well
91:06 bad switch
91:07 buy desk
91:08 paid his wife
91:09 bad soup
91:10 bad days
91:11 potato head
91:12 bite down
91:13 bed time
91:14 bad odor
91:15 paid toll
91:16 bad dish
92:01 poinsettia
92:02 happy in sun
92:03 pains me
92:04 pains her
92:05 pencil
92:06 opens show
92:07 been sick
92:08 open safe
92:09 bounce up
92:10 pants

92:11 bandit
92:12 happy Indian
92:13 bantam
92:14 painter
92:15 ponytail
93:01 bombs it
93:02 up the Amazon
93:03 bombs them
93:04 bombs her
93:05 bombs wall
94:01 priest
94:02 person
94:03 bruise him
94:04 appraiser
94:05 Brazil
94:06 power switch
94:07 brisk
94:08 pours half
94:09 bar is up
94:10 pirates
94:11 braided
94:12 baritone
94:13 boredom
94:14 braid hair
94:15 bridle
94:16 Broadway show
94:17 boardwalk
94:18 borrow a TV
94:19 pretty boy
94:20 prunes
94:21 burnt
94:22 pronoun
94:23 brown ham
95:01 pool side
95:02 bless wine
95:03 bless him
95:04 blazer
95:05 please all
95:06 please wash
95:07 please go
95:08 plays off
95:09 bless boy
95:10 plates
95:11 pleated
96:01 hope chest
96:02 pushes on

96:03 pushes me
96:04 pushes her
96:05 patches hole
96:06 bashes show
96:07 pushes guy
96:08 pushes off
96:09 pushes up
96:10 beach days
96:11 pushed ahead
96:12 beach town
96:13 pushed him
97:01 back seat
97:02 backs in
97:03 buxom
97:04 boxer
97:05 packs well
97:06 packs shoe
97:07 back is weak
97:08 backs off
97:09 picks up
97:10 pockets
97:11 polka dot
97:12 backed in
98:01 happy feast
98:02 above sun
98:03 above his home
98:04 buy VCR
98:05 paves well
98:06 buffs watch
98:07 buff rug
98:08 pay off his wife
98:09 buffs up
99:01 baby sit
99:02 pops in
99:03 baby's home
99:04 baby's hair
99:05 baby's well
99:06 baby's age
99:07 baby is awake
99:08 pops off
99:09 Papa's boy
100:01 wet, he says stay
100:02 daisies sun
100:03 daisies swim
100:04 daisies soar
100:05 daisies sell

101:01 dusty city
101:02 wet citizen
101:03 twist some
101:04 twist, sir
101:05 twist, silly
101:06 dusty switch
101:07 wet, stays awake
101:08 dusty sofa
102:01 wet snowsuit
102:02 wet, see Hawaiian sun
102:03 wet, suns me
102:04 wet, sincere
102:05 wet, suns oil
102:06 wet, sneeze - achu
102:07 wet, sun soak
102:08 wet, snow is heavy
102:09 wet, sun's up
102:10 wet, sunny days
102:11 wet, sunny today
102:12 wet suntan
102:13 wet house and home
102:14 wet snowtire
102:15 wet sundial
102:16 wet sandwich
102:17 wet San Diego
102:18 wet, Sony TV
102:19 wet, sunny top
102:20 wet, use onions
102:21 wet, sign note
102:22 wet, CNN on
102:23 wet, sign name
102:24 wet, sign in here
102:25 wet, CNN will
102:26 wet, sunny, enjoy
102:27 wet, sunning
102:28 wet, sane Navy
103:01 wet swim suit
103:02 wet, wise mason
103:03 wet, see museum
103:04 wet, wise miser
103:05 wet, icy muzzle
103:06 wet, same switch
103:07 wet, hazy mask
103:08 wet some sofa
103:09 wet, his mishap
103:10 wet housemates

103:11 wet, swim to it
103:12 wet, his hometown
103:13 wet sometime
103:14 wet cemetery
103:15 wet, icy metal
103:16 wet, use my dish
103:17 wet, use my deck
103:18 wet, zoom TV
103:19 wet, Yes! a mudpie
103:20 wet, summons
103:21 wet cement
103:22 wet iceman won
104:01 wet, house arrest
104:02 wet, hazy Arizona
104:03 wet his resume
104:04 wet, sorry sir
104:05 wet, yes, wrestle
104:06 wet, see her switch
104:07 wet his rescue
104:08 wet, see her sofa
104:09 wet, his hour is up
104:10 wet, house riots
104:11 wet, I swore today
104:12 wet, see her tan
104:13 wet, his red home
104:14 wet, icy radar
104:15 wet, sore tail
104:16 wet, sour dish
104:17 wet, icy, red key
104:18 wet, see her TV
104:19 wet, he's read up
104:20 wet sirens
104:21 wet serenade
104:22 wet, sour onion
104:23 wet, see her name
104:24 wet, see runner
104:25 wet, ice, rain, hail
104:26 wet his ranch
104:27 wet, soaring
104:28 wet, sour enough
104:29 wet, he's run by
104:30 wet, icy rooms
104:31 wet, sorry mate
104:32 wet ceremony
104:33 wet, sorry Mom
104:34 wet house warmer

104:35 wet, sorry meal
105:01 wet, he's lost
105:02 wet, slow zone
105:03 wet, a seal swam
105:04 wet, has lovely hair
105:05 wet, sells oil
105:06 wet, sells shoe
105:07 wet, see Alaska
105:08 wet, sails off
105:09 wet, slows up
105:10 wet slides
105:11 wet, sold it
105:12 wet, slow down
105:13 wet, sold home
105:14 wet, salute her
105:15 wet, salad oil
105:16 wet, sold watch
105:17 wet, sell dog
105:18 wet, sold off
105:19 wet, seal it up
105:20 wet saloons
105:21 wet Iceland
105:22 wet swollen knee
105:23 wet, slain him
105:24 wet, slain her
105:25 wet salon oil
105:26 wet, icy lunch
105:27 wet sailing
105:28 wet, sell knife
105:29 wet, has the line-up
105:30 wet, slams
105:31 wet soulmate
105:32 wet, silly man
105:33 wet, sell my home
105:34 wet, silly hammer
105:35 wet, seal mail
105:36 wet, sell my shoe
105:37 wet, slum week
105:38 wet, silly movie
105:39 wet, slump
105:40 wet sellers
105:41 wet sleigh ride
105:42 wet, silly run
105:43 wet, sell rum
105:44 wet, silly roar
105:45 wet, slower whale

106:01 wet, ice chest
106:02 wet, switch is on
106:03 wet, switches ham
106:04 wet, switches hour
106:05 wet ice chisel
106:06 wet, switches shoe
106:07 wet, switch sock
106:08 wet, switch is off
106:09 wet, switches soap
106:10 wet, see jets
106:11 wet, switched tea
106:12 wet, switched on
106:13 wet, switch team
106:14 wet, ice shatter
106:15 wet, switch towel
106:16 wet, switch dish
106:17 wet, switch dog
106:18 wet, switched off
106:19 wet, switched pie
106:20 wet, icy chains
106:21 wet, switch hand
106:22 wet, see China now
106:23 wet, switch name
106:24 wet, switch owner
106:25 wet, switch nail
106:26 wet, see a change
106:27 wet, switching
106:28 wet, switch knife
106:29 hits a change-up
106:30 hits a huge mouse
106:31 wet, was she mad
106:32 douse a huge man
106:33 wet, switch mummy
106:34 wet, switch hammer
106:35 wet, switch mail
106:36 wet, switch match
106:37 wet, switch mug
106:38 wet, switch movie
106:39 wet, switch map
106:40 wet his jersey
106:41 wet his shirt
106:42 wet his journey
106:43 wet his germ
106:44 dosage, roar
106:45 wet, switch rail
106:46 wet his church

106:47 dizzy shark
106:48 dizzy sheriff
107:01 wet, squeezed
107:02 dizzy cousin
107:03 desk is home
107:04 desk is here
107:05 wet, ski icy hill
107:06 wet, soaks wash
107:07 wet zig zag
107:08 wet, squeeze wife
107:09 too high - sky is up
107:10 wet skits
107:11 wet, skated
107:12 wet, ski down
107:13 desk time
107:14 hot skater
107:15 hits cattle
107:16 wet, soak dish
107:17 wet, sick dog
107:18 desk, TV
107:19 dizzy, get up
107:20 wet skins
107:21 ate his candy
107:22 wet, skin knee
107:23 wet, skinny Ma
107:24 hot scanner
107:25 wet, icy canal
107:26 wet, skinny shoe
107:27 dizzy king
107:28 wet, skinny half
107:29 wet, ski on by
107:30 wet, skims
107:31 wet, soak meat
107:32 wet, sick man
107:33 wet, sick Mom
107:34 desk, hammer
107:35 desk meal
107:36 wet, sick match
107:37 wet, soggy, muggy
107:38 disco movie
107:39 wet, skimpy
107:40 wet cigars
107:41 wet cigarette
107:42 wet screen
107:43 eat ice cream
108:01 wet sofa seat

108:02 wet, save the sun
108:03 hat saves me
108:04 hat saves her
108:05 wet, sea fossil
108:06 wet, saves wash
108:07 dizzy fiasco
108:08 wet, safe, safe
108:09 heat saves up
108:10 dizzy videos
108:11 wet, soft head
108:12 deceived hen
108:13 the heat saved me
109:01 dizzy boys ate
109:02 wets basin
109:03 dizzy boys hum
109:04 hot soup is here
109:05 hot soup is oily
109:06 wet, see boys itch
109:07 hot soup is weak
109:08 days by his wife
109:09 wet, soaps up
109:10 wets the beds
109:11 wets potato
109:12 wets button
109:13 wet, sip it Ma
109:14 wet spider
109:15 wet hospital
109:16 wet, soapy dish
109:17 heats paddock
109:18 dispute with wife
109:19 wet, speed by
109:20 head spins
109:21 heats paint
109:22 heats up onion
109:23 heats up gnome
109:24 wet, spin hair
109:25 wet, spin wool
109:26 wet spinach
109:27 wet, sipping
109:28 hat spun off
109:29 tie spun by
109:30 dizzy bombs
109:31 dizzy, bombed
110:01 die, deceased
110:02 wet, wet season
110:03 wet, it's so homey

110:04 wet, it was sorry
110:05 wet, it's so oily
110:06 wet, it's so chewy
110:07 wet, it's sick
111:01 wet, dead city
110:02 wet, die too soon
111:03 wet, dates me
111:04 wet, today's weather
111:05 wet, wet tassel
111:06 wet, Dad's watch
111:07 wet, today is OK
111:08 wet, date is off
111:09 wet, heated soup
111:10 wet, eat toads
112:01 wet, twin city
112:03 wet, a tiny sum
112:04 wet, dinosaur
112:05 wet, tonsil
112:06 wet, twins age
112:07 wet, tiny sock
112:08 wet, what a nice wife
112:09 wet, tunes up
112:10 wet, doughnuts
113:01 wet, die, homicide
113:02 wet, time is now
113:03 wet, hit the museum
113:04 wet, do you miss her
113:05 wet, hid the missile
113:06 wet, time his wash
113:07 wet, tummy sick
113:08 wet, hide my safe
113:09 wet, eat my soup
114:01 wet, trust
114:02 wet, treason
114:03 wet, dries him
114:04 wet, dresser
114:05 wet, drizzle
114:06 wet, dressage
114:07 wet, to the rescue
114:08 wet, dries off
115:01 wet, deal set
115:02 wet, dials in
115:03 wet, tails him
115:04 wet, Dolly's here
115:05 wet, till soil
115:06 wet, dials shoe

115:07 wet, white Alaska
115:08 wet, tells off
115:09 wet, dials up
115:10 wet, toilets
115:11 wet, diluted
115:12 wet, dial tone
115:13 wet, tell it, Ma
115:14 wet, tall door
115:15 wet, tall tale
115:16 wet, tall dish
115:17 wet, tall dog
115:18 wet, tall TV
116:01 wet, digest
116:02 wet, touch the sun
116:03 wet, touches him
116:04 wet, touches her
116:05 wet, teach us well
116:06 wet, dishes wash
116:07 wet, teach us, OK
116:08 wet, touch sofa
116:09 wet, touches up
116:10 wet sheets
116:11 wet, dish it out
116:12 wet, touchdown
116:13 wet, it shot him
116:14 wet, white shutter
116:15 wet, dish towel
116:16 wet, touch dish
116:17 wet, touch dog
116:18 wet, touch TV
116:19 wet, touch it up
117:01 wet, tuxedo
117:02 wet, hit casino
118:01 wet, TV set
118:02 wet, TV is on
118:03 wet, TV zoom
118:04 wet, tough sir
118:05 wet, hide fossil
118:06 wet, TV switch
118:07 wet, TV is sick
118:08 wet, TV is off
118:09 wet, tough soap
118:10 wet, divots
118:11 wet, divided
118:12 wet, out of town
118:13 wet, dive team

118:14 wet, tough tire
118:15 wet, TV dial
118:16 wet, divide wash
118:17 wet, Daffy Duck
118:18 wet, tough, tough
118:19 wet, divide by
118:20 wet, advance
118:21 wet, defined
118:22 wet, tough Nun
118:23 wet, dive on him
118:24 wet, divine hair
118:25 wet, tough nail
118:26 wet, divine witch
118:27 wet, diving
118:28 wet, TV on/off
118:29 wet, divine hope
119:01 wet, deposit
119:02 wet, eat poison
119:03 wet, tips him
119:04 wet, tips her
119:05 wet topsoil
119:06 wet, tips a witch
119:07 wet, toupee is a wig
119:08 wet, tipsy wife
119:09 wet, hit the busboy
119:10 wet, diabetes
119:11 hot, hot potato
119:12 wet, deep down
119:13 wet, top team
119:14 wet, tap water
119:15 wet, top hotel
119:16 wet, top dish
119:17 wet, tape deck
119:18 wet, deep dive
119:19 wet, tip top
119:20 wet, head pains
119:21 wet, deep end
119:22 wet, eat banana
119:23 wet, top name
119:24 wet, top owner
119:25 wet pinwheel
119:26 wet, hit - punch
119:27 wet, tipping
119:28 wet, tip knife
119:29 wet, top knob
119:30 wet, wet palms

119:31 wet, tie up meat
119:32 wet, tie up man
119:33 wet, tie up Mom
119:34 wet, dip more
119:35 wet, tie up mail
119:36 wet, top match
119:37 wet, tip mug
119:38 wet, top movie
119:39 wet heat pump
119:40 wet, depress
119:41 wet tea party
119:42 wet, white - brown
119:43 wet tapeworm
119:44 wet, hit barrier
119:45 wet, top rail
119:46 wet, white brush
119:47 wet, wet park
119:48 wet, deprive
119:49 wet, eat - burp
119:50 wet tables
119:51 wet tablet
119:52 wet, Dublin
119:53 wet, diploma
119:54 wet, dip lower
119:55 wet, hit blue whale
119:56 wet, hot blush
119:57 wet, diabolic
119:58 wet, double off
119:59 hot, hot apple pie
119:60 wet, wet bushes
119:61 wet bushy head
119:62 wet, hot passion
119:63 wet, tip jam
119:64 wet, tip chair
119:65 wet, eat a bushel
119:66 wet, top judge
119:67 wet, tip the shake
119:68 wet, top chef
119:69 wet, top shape
119:70 wet, tea bags
119:71 wet topcoat
119:72 wet toboggan
119:73 wet, top game
119:74 woody woodpecker
119:75 wet, white buckle
119:76 wet, top coach

119:77 wet, dab cookie
119:78 wet, tip coffee
119:79 wet, tip cup
119:80 wet, dab face
119:81 wet, top video
119:82 wet, heat up oven
119:83 wet, tape foam
119:84 wet, tip over
119:85 wet, top of hill
119:86 wet, dopey fish
119:87 wet, top half, OK
119:88 wet, hit above ivy
119:89 wet, tip the FBI
119:90 wet, tip bus
119:91 wet, tip boat
119:92 wet, tip piano
119:93 wet, dip palm
119:94 wet, white paper
119:95 wet, wet bubble
119:96 wet, wet baby wash
119:97 wet, tip bike
119:98 wet, tip above
119:99 wet, hit a pop-up
119:100 Dad bites ice
119:101 Dad, Pizza Hut
119:102 Dad, bad sun
119:103 Dad, potassium
119:104 Dad, Budweiser
119:105 Dad, beats well
119:106 Dad, bad switch
119:107 Dad, buy desk
119:108 Dad, paid his wife
119:109 Dad, bad soup
119:110 Dad, bad days
119:111 Dad, potato head
119:112 Dad, bite down
119:113 Dad, bed time
119:114 Dad, bad odor
119:115 Dad paid toll
119:116 Dad, bad dish
119:117 Dad, Dad, bad dog
119:118 Dad, bad TV
119:119 Dad, potato pie
119:120 Dad, buttons
119:121 Dad buttoned
119:122 Dad, bad onion

119:123 Dad, bad name
119:124 Dad, boutonniere
119:125 Dad bought a nail
119:126 Dad, bad nacho
119:127 Dad, biting
119:128 Dad beat Navy
119:129 Dad, button up
119:130 Dad, bottoms
119:131 Dad, bottom out
119:132 Dad, Batman
119:133 Dad, beat Miami
119:134 Dad bought more
119:135 Dad, bad meal
119:136 Dad, bad match
119:137 Dad bought a mug
119:138 Dad, bad movie
119:139 Dad beat him up
119:140 Dad powders
119:141 Dad buttered
119:142 Dad better win
119:143 Dad, bad aroma
119:144 Dad, better hair
119:145 Dad, butter, oil
119:146 Dad, better show
119:147 Dad, buy truck
119:148 Dad, paid her off
119:149 Dad, batter up
119:150 Dad, beetles
119:151 Dad, paddled
119:152 Dad, battalion
119:153 Dad, battle hymn
119:154 Dad, bad lawyer
119:155 Dad, paddle wheel
119:156 Dad, bite leash
119:157 Dad, bad leg
119:158 Dad, bad love
119:159 Dad, bite lip
119:160 Dad, bad cheese
119:161 Dad, bad shot
119:162 Dad, beautician
119:163 Dad bought a gym
119:164 Dad, badger
119:165 Dad, bad jail
119:166 Dad, bad judge
119:167 Dad, bad check
119:168 Dad, bad chef

119:169 **Dad, pet shop**
119:170 **Dad, pay tax**
119:171 **Dad, beat egg white**
119:172 **Dad, beauty queen**
119:173 **Dad, bad game**
119:174 **Dad, pit crew**
119:175 **Dad, bad call**
119:176 **Dad paid cash**
120:01 wet **honey is sweet**
120:02 wet, **nice son**
120:03 wet, **knows his math**
120:04 wet, **necessary**
120:05 wet, **nice sale**
120:06 wet, **nice switch**
120:07 wet, **niece is weak**
121:01 wet, **window seat**
121:02 wet, **end zone**
121:03 wet, **handsome**
121:04 wet, **needs her**
121:05 wet, **window sill**
121:06 wet, **window sash**
121:07 wet, **new desk**
121:08 wet, **need a sofa**
122:01 wet, **Nuns eat**
122:02 wet, **no, no son**
122:03 wet, **in a nice home**
122:04 wet, **Nuns hair**
122:05 wet, **no nozzle**
122:06 **tiny nice watch**
122:07 wet, **Nun is awake**
122:08 wet, **Nun is heavy**
122:09 wet, **onion soup**
123:01 wet, **no mist**
123:02 wet, **no my son**
123:03 wet, **new museum**
123:04 wet, **no miser**
124:01 wet, **unrest**
124:02 wet, **in Arizona**
124:03 wet, **honors me**
124:04 wet, **nursery**
124:05 wet, **no resale**
124:06 wet, **owners wish**
124:07 wet, **no rescue**
124:08 wet, **New Year's Eve**
125:01 wet, **win lawsuit**
125:02 wet, **kneel son**

125:03 wet, **nails them**
125:04 wet, **new laser**
125:05 wet, **nails wall**
126:01 wet, **unjust**
126:02 wet, **unchosen**
126:03 wet, **nachos - yum!**
126:04 **tiny chaser**
126:05 wet, **when she's well**
126:06 wet, **when she's shy**
127:01 wet, **no guest**
127:02 wet, **Yankees win**
127:03 wet, **wings me away**
127:04 wet, **Yankees hour**
127:05 wet, **in a castle**
128:01 wet, **invest**
128:02 wet, **naive son**
128:03 wet, **envies them**
128:04 wet, **no officer**
128:05 wet, **Navy Seal**
128:06 wet, **on/off switch**
129:01 wet, **no pest**
129:02 wet, **no poison**
129:03 wet, **no buys..hmmm**
129:04 wet, **unbusy hour**
129:05 wet, **new puzzle**
129:06 wet, **unhappy switch**
129:07 wet, **knapsack**
129:08 wet, **now pass off**
130:01 wet, **misused**
130:02 wet, **Miss USA won**
130:03 wet, **misses him**
130:04 wet, **I'm so sorry**
130:05 wet, **misses a wheel**
130:06 wet, **misses a shoe**
130:07 wet, **I'm so sick**
130:08 wet, **I'm so safe**
131:01 wet, **midwest**
131:02 wet, **medicine**
131:03 wet, **meets him**
132:01 wet, **Minnesota**
132:02 wet, **monsoon**
132:03 wet, **mini swim**
132:04 wet, **menswear**
132:05 wet, **mean seal**
132:06 wet, **women's watch**
132:07 wet, **women's wig**

132:08 wet, **man's wife**
132:09 wet, **minesweep**
132:10 wet, **mints**
132:11 wet, **mandate**
132:12 wet, **mountain**
132:13 wet, **menu item**
132:14 wet, **monitor**
132:15 wet, **mantel**
132:16 wet, **main dish**
132:17 wet, **mean dog**
132:18 wet, **minute off**
133:01 hot, **Miami's hot**
133:02 ate **Mom's honey**
133:03 heat **Mom's home**
134:01 hit **Mayor's aide**
134:02 hot, **more sun**
134:03 time her swim
135:01 wet, **I'm lost**
135:02 hot, **I'm loose now**
135:03 hit you, **mauls him**
135:04 hot mail is here
135:05 hot meal is well
135:06 hot meal is chewy
135:07 hot meal is OK
135:08 hot mail is off
135:09 hot mail swap
135:10 hot melodies
135:11 wet, **melted**
135:12 would you mail it in
135:13 wet, **melt me**
135:14 wet, **mild weather**
135:15 wet, **melt hill**
135:16 wet, **melt shoe**
135:17 wet mile to go
135:18 wet, **mild wave**
135:19 wet, **I'm laid up**
135:20 hot melons
135:21 wet melon head
136:01 I hate majesty
136:02 hot match is on
136:03 heat matches him
136:04 heat matches her
136:05 heat my chisel
136:06 wet matches, shoe
136:07 wet, **match sock**
136:08 wet match is off

136:09 wet **match** is up
136:10 **timesheets**
136:11 hot, **I'm shut** out
136:12 wet, **I'm shut** in
136:13 **dumb showtime**
136:14 **dim shutter**
136:15 heat my **huge deal**
136:16 wet **mash dish**
136:17 heat my **huge deck**
136:18 too **much TV**
136:19 **hood matched** up
136:20 hot **machines**
136:21 **dumb giant**
136:22 hot, **may I join** in
136:23 hot, **match name**
136:24 wet **machinery**
136:25 **dumb channel**
136:26 **time change**
137:01 **dumb guest**
137:02 **dumb cousin**
137:03 **tomahawks me**
137:04 **tomahawks her**
137:05 **tomahawks all**
137:06 **tomahawks shoe**
137:07 hot **Mexico**
137:08 **tomahawks sofa**
137:09 **tomahawks subway**
138:01 **dumb feast**
138:02 at the **movies now**
138:03 **Ed moves home**
138:04 **time off**, sir
138:05 **dumb fossil**
138:06 hot **movies, watch**
138:07 hot **movie is OK**
138:08 hot **movie is off**
139:01 **dumps wood**
139:02 a **damp sign**
139:03 **dumps home**
139:04 **damps hair**
139:05 **dumps whale**
139:06 **dumps wash**
139:07 **dumps wig**
139:08 **dumps half**
139:09 **dumps pie**
139:10 wet, **empty house**
139:11 wet, **emptied**

139:12 **dumped wine**
139:13 **damp dime**
139:14 **damp door**
139:15 **damp towel**
139:16 wet, **empty shoe**
139:17 **damp dog**
139:18 **damp TV**
139:19 **damp teepee**
139:20 **damp nose**
139:21 **damp net**
139:22 **damp onion**
139:23 **dump name**
139:24 hot **wiener**
140:01 **dries his head**
140:02 **dry season**
140:03 he **tries some**
140:04 wet **rice, sir**
140:05 **dries sail**
140:06 **dries his wash**
140:07 **deer is sick**
140:08 **deer is safe**
140:09 **door is soapy**
140:10 **dries toes**
140:11 wet, **rusted**
140:12 **dry stone**
140:13 **dry stem**
141:01 **dried seed**
141:02 **trade son**
141:03 **dried his ham**
141:04 **dried his hair**
141:05 wet **yard sale**
141:06 **dried his wash**
141:07 wet **red sock**
141:08 **dried his wife**
141:09 **dried soap**
141:10 wet **rodeo days**
142:01 **train is wide**
142:02 **drowns hen**
142:03 **trains him**
142:04 **train is here**
142:05 **drains well**
142:06 **drains shoe**
142:07 **drains egg**
143:01 wet **or misty**
143:02 **true mason**
143:03 a **tire museum**

143:04 **true miser**
143:05 try a **muzzle**
143:06 try her **massage**
143:07 try **music**
143:08 **drum is heavy**
143:09 **true mess up**
143:10 hot **remedies**
143:11 **dream died**
143:12 **trim, tiny**
144:01 **terrorist**
144:02 **dry raisin**
144:03 **dry résumé**
144:04 wet her **razor**
144:05 wet **rehearsal**
144:06 **dry her switch**
144:07 **water rescue**
144:08 try her **sofa**
144:09 try her **soap**
144:10 **dry her toes**
144:11 wet, **rewrite it**
144:12 **terror town**
144:13 **terror team**
144:14 **wide rear door**
144:15 wet your **rattle**
145:01 wet, **really sweet**
145:02 **trial is on**
145:03 wet, **roll, swim**
145:04 **trail is here**
145:05 wet, **really silly**
145:06 wet **rail switch**
145:07 **try Alaska**
145:08 **trial is off**
145:09 **trial soap**
145:10 **true ladies**
145:11 **troll died**
145:12 wet, **roll down**
145:13 wet, **real dumb**
145:14 hot **realtor**
145:15 wet, **worldly**
145:16 **truly touchy**
145:17 **trail dog**
145:18 **truly tough**
145:19 wet, **roll the tape**
145:20 **true lines**
145:21 a **trillion hid**
146:01 **trashes hut**

146:02 wet, reach the sun
146:03 trashes home
146:04 heat reaches her
146:05 trashes well
146:06 trashes shoe
146:07 trashes wig
146:08 trashes ivy
146:09 heat reaches up
146:10 trash days
147:01 drags hat
147:02 treks in
147:03 treks home
147:04 tracks her
147:05 dry castle
147:06 drags shoe
147:07 drags wig
147:08 drags ivy
147:09 dry gazebo
147:10 wet rockets
147:11 dragged tie
147:12 dry kitten
147:13 drag dime
147:14 tractor
147:15 drag towel
147:16 dragged wash
147:17 drag dog
147:18 dragged off
147:19 trekked up
147:20 dragons

148:01 drives it
148:02 drives on
148:03 drives home
148:04 drives her
148:05 drives well
148:06 drives Joe
148:07 wet roof is OK
148:08 drives off
148:09 drives up
148:10 wet rivets
148:11 drove Dad
148:12 wet, rough town
148:13 had a rough time
148:14 hit rough water
149:01 drops hat
149:02 drops in
149:03 drops ham
149:04 drapes hair
149:05 dry puzzle
149:06 drops shoe
149:07 drops wig
149:08 drops off
149:09 drop soap
150:01 deal is set
150:02 tells his son
150:03 tells his Ma
150:04 dolls soar
150:05 wet, loose soil
150:06 tells his age

Questions and Answers on the Phonetic Alphabet

Q: Am I expected to comprehend all those columns from page 51 to 77?

A: No. What is required is to be able to comprehend the table (pages 45-50). It's imperative that you know the number/consonant code.

Q: How much time will this take to master that coding system?

A: It shouldn't take much time at all. Focus on the hints, such as 3M Company and that a turned m̲ resembles a 3. Four ends with the letter *R*, and the letter n̲ has 2 downstrokes. Soon, you'll able to know which number (0-9) codes to which sound.

Q: Isn't there an easier way to do this?

A: No, only because we're dealing with thousands and thousands of numbers. By utilizing the phonetic alphabet we're now able to put a visual or phrase to each number. This gives us a tremendous advantage to remembering.

Q: Can you give examples using Chapter 1, Verse 2 for John, 1 John, 2 John, 3 John?

A: Chapter 1, Verse 2 equals 1:2, and 1:2 equals tuna (see page 51). The tuna must come into play for each of the 4 books in your question. Remember, *t* is 1, and *n* is 2. If we fail to place the tuna into the picture we will not know that it's Chapter 1, Verse 2.

John 1:2 codes to toilet paper roll and tuna. Remember, the toilet paper came from the John.

John 1:2 reads ... He was with God in the beginning.

The key words are *God* and *Beginning*. We now have a book to remember, a chapter and verse to remember, and the scripture to remember. Remembering three separate things can be difficult. Fortunately, there's an easy way.

Imagine a tuna juggling or unraveling or holding toilet paper. When we see that one image, we instantly know that it's John 1:2. All we need is to place the scripture into the scene. Imagine the tuna is unraveling the toilet paper and on the first square is God or a Guard which reminds us of God. God is on the beginning square.

In that one image we see the tuna unraveling toilet paper and God is on the beginning square and He was with God in the beginning. That one image tells us that it's John 1:2 and the scripture is *He was with God in the beginning.*

Q: Doesn't this belittle the Bible?

A: Just the contrary. It reinforces God's Word into our brains. That silly picture only acts as a reminder for us to say, "Oh yeah, I remember that scripture." And, remembering is our goal.

Q: What about 1 John, 2 John, and 3 John? Won't that be confusing if we want to recall Chapter 1, Verse 2 for each one?

A: Referring back to page 24, we see the image for 1 John is an outhouse with one half-moon. Once we visualize a tuna squeezing through that half-moon, we already know that we're going to be focused on 1 John 1:2.

1 John 1:2 reads ... The life appeared; we have seen it and testify to it, and we proclaim to you the eternal life, which was with the Father and has appeared to us.

The key word is *eternal*. Imagine a tuna, squeezed through the half-moon of an outhouse, is turning (sounds like eternal, as in e-turn-al) that half-moon. To remember the beginning of the scripture we can imagine that the tuna begins to lift a pear as it turns the half-moon. The words *lift* and *pear* are similar to *life* and *a-pear-ed*.

Q: Okay, what about 2 John 1:2. Can you explain that?

A: Once again, referring back to page 24, we see that the visual code for 2 John is a bathtub with 2 handles. Those 2 handles in the bathtub, which is located in the John, can only mean 2 John. And once again, a tuna must be in the scene to know that it's Chapter 1, Verse 2.

2 John 1:2 reads ... because of the truth, which lives in us and will be with us forever.

The key words are *truth* and *forever*. Imagine a tuna, sitting in the bathtub, with a huge tooth. He tries to remove his tooth using great force (as in 4-orce, reminding us it's 4-ever). That one image tells us the book, the chapter and verse, and the scripture.

NOTE: There will be no confusion if we're in the Book of Ruth since Tooth is that image. Each image of Ruth takes place in our mouths, whereas the image for this tooth takes place in the bathtub (2 John).

Q: What can you tell us about 3 John 1:2?

A: Referring back to page 24, we see the image for 3 John is an electric razor with 3 dials. That razor, along with the tuna, must be in the same scene.

3 John 1:2 reads ... Dear Friend, I pray that you enjoy good health and that all may go well with you, even as your soul is getting along well.

Key word is *health*. Imagine my dear friend, the tuna is using an electric razor on its heal, with *heal* sounding like *health*. This visual reminds us that the scripture is about *health*.

Q: It takes practice, doesn't it?

A: Use this system to remember 10 Bible Verses in the next 3 days. You'll be amazed at your progress.

PATHWAYS
FOR
REMEMBERING

On the following pages there 25 examples of putting it all together to remember the Book, Chapter and Verse, and Scripture.

We'll use the VINE system (see page 8) to connect these 3 parts.

Visual

Each book will be visualized using the pictures from page 14 - 24. If it's in the Book of Amos we'll use an arrow; the Book of Habakkuk we'll use a hubcap; the Book of Colossians we'll use a column; if it's in the Book of Philemon we'll use a gasoline pump; and if it's in the Book of Titus we'll use a rope.

Each Chapter and Verse will be exchanged to the corresponding number from the phonetic alphabet directory (pages 51 – 77).

If the Chapter and Verse is 9:12, we'll turn to the directory and see that 9:12 codes to a *button*. Then, we'll connect button to the specific Book.

If it's 26:40 we'll see that it codes to *New Jersey*. Then, we'll connect New Jersey to the specific book. Whether we visualize the State of New Jersey or a brand new jersey it makes no difference. It's imperative however, that the New Jersey must be connected to the book.

If it's in Titus, we can visualize a rope wrapped around the State of New Jersey or a rope wrapped around a new jersey.

If it's in Habakkuk, we can visualize hubcaps rolling into New Jersey or a brand new jersey wrapped around a hubcap.

If it's in 2 Thessalonians, which is represented by scissors, we can visualize the State of New Jersey is cut in half by giant scissors or we're taking scissors to our brand new jersey.

If the Chapter and Verse is 26:39, we'll turn back to the pages of the directory and see that the number codes to *no shampoo*.

If it's in Titus, we can visualize that the rope is inside an empty shampoo bottle and then the rope realizes that there's <u>no shampoo</u>. If it's in Philemon, we can visualize that we're trying to get shampoo into the gas tank, but there's <u>no shampoo</u>.

Fortunately, there will never be any *no shampoo* in both Titus and Philemon because the former book only goes up to Chapter 1, Verse 15, and the latter book extends to only Chapter 1, Verse 25.

So far, we can now visualize each of the 66 Books, and put an image to each number, but what about the scripture? We may not see any visuals. At first glance, you may not see any visual, but God works in mysterious ways and every word can be broken down and tweaked to give us a glimpse of hope that there really is something there.

The word *but* can be visualized to a cigarette *butt* or a kick in the *butt*. The word *And* sounds like *hand* and that can be visualized. The word *his* sounds like *hiss* which is a sound a snake emits.

The word *can* be visualized to a *soup can*. The word *together* sounds like *tooth-gether*, and that can be visualized. The word *for* sounds like *floor*; the word *I* becomes an *Eye*, and the word *was* is only a letter off to becoming a *wasp*.

That becomes a *hat*; *of* becomes an *oven*, and *which* becomes a *witch*. *Thee* becomes a *tree*; *you* is now a *ewe*, and *our* is an *hourglass*. The word *in* becomes an *inn*, *want* is an *ant*, and *according* is an *accordion*.

Will this take you off track from what you want to remember? <u>Abdomen knot!!!!!</u> translated to ... absolutely not!

The visual will keep you from falling off the track. The picture will be a gentle reminder for you to stay on course to recall the verse. Study the 25 examples beginning on page 87 to see how it works.

Imagination

Einstein said that logic takes you from A to Z, whereas imagination takes you everywhere. To recall these verses, one must tap into their imagination juices. To enhance these images, try to enlarge what you want to remember.

On the preceeding page, did you make note that it wasn't only a pair of scissors cutting into New Jersey, but it was <u>giant</u> scissors? To imbed that image into our minds we could have used hundreds of scissors cutting into New Jersey. Whoever uttered the phrase, 'the more the merrier' was only half right. It should be, 'the more the memorable.'

<u>Disclaimer</u>: To my friends in New Jersey, don't despair. Scissors will never cut into your beautiful state because 2 Thessalonians only extends to Chapter 3, Verse 18. But be on the alert; a <u>*mid-wife*</u> is holding scissors.

Neighborhood

You'll see in the 25 examples that key words are pulled out of the scripture. Finding these key words will help in remembering the scripture. Perhaps you don't want to memorize every single word within the passage, but only want to retain the scripture's meaning. Getting those key words from out of the neighborhood of the scripture will help.

Exaggeration

To recall these 3 areas of the Bible (Book, Chapter and Verse, and Scripture), we must put them all into an intersection. We want to see one and be reminded of the other two. There is no other way to do that unless we exaggerate the image.

In the 25 examples, exaggeration is key because it forces us to remember. Keep an open mind when reading these examples and unleash your imagination. Unleash it to remember any verse in the Bible. Use that imagination that God gave you and develop it.

PUTTING IT ALL TOGETHER

- 25 examples -

James 3:17-18 / But the wisdom that comes from heaven is first of all pure, then peace-loving, considerate, submissive, full of mercy and good fruit, impartial and sincere. Peacemakers who sow in peace raise a harvest of righteousness.

Breaking down the scripture

Jam, **MeDiC** = James 3:17. Visualize a *MEDIC* putting a bandage on a jar of *JAM*. This image tells us that it's James 3:17.

The bandage, which represents a medic, is on the BUTT end of the jam. This reminds us that the word *But* begins the scripture.

The next key word is *wisdom*. Imagine the Jam sitting atop the W. The W is holding up the jar of jam. The W reminds us that the word is *wisdom*.

Book - **James**

Chapter & Verses – Bandage applied by MEDIC – 3:17

Scripture – Wisdom …

The next key word is *comes*. Note the similarity of the last three letters (m e s) of *James* and *Comes*. This helps us remember.

But the wisdom that comes from heaven is first of all pure,

The words *from* and *first* both have the *f r* sound which aids us in remembering. Imagine jam that is coming from the heaven that is *all pure*.

But the wisdom that comes from heaven is first of all pure, then peace-loving,

After the word *pure* the next key word is *peace-loving*. Both words start with the letter *p*. The next consonant sound in *peace* is the letter

87

<u>c</u>, which brings us to <u>c</u>onsiderate.

... considerate, submissive, full of mercy and good fruit, Think of a con man who goes down (sub). Another clue is that the letter after con is <u>s</u>, which leads to *submissive*. Submissive is similar to submarine. A submarine goes full speed ahead. The word *full* follows sub-submissive. The next key words are *good fruit*. Jam is good fruit.

... full of mercy and good fruit, impartial and sincere

Think of a good fruit that is partially eaten. When Eve ate the forbidden fruit she sinned. Sinned and sin begin with the same sound.

Run the words *impartial and sincere* together. It's easier to recall when it's written as, 'impartialandsincere.' The words roll off our tongues.

... impartial and sincere. Peacemakers who sow in peace raise a harvest of righteousness.

The word *sincere* is similar to *Sincerely*, which is written on pieces of paper. *Sincere* and *Peace* are now linked.

Visualize *sewing* a *piece* of cloth and *raising* it on a flagpole.

The words *raise, harvest* and *righteousness* have an <u>r</u> present. The connection helps us remember the rest of the verse.

You could also visualize a harvest (harvest) of raisins (raise) that's just right (righteousness).

But the wisdom that comes from heaven is first of all pure, then peace-loving, considerate, submissive, full of mercy and good fruit, impartial and sincere. Peacemakers who sow in peace raise a harvest of righteousness.

Read the verse slowly and think about the meaning ...

Matthew 22:37 / Jesus replied, Love the Lord your God with all your heart and with all your soul and with all your mind.

Breaking down the scripture

Door Mat, u**N**io**N** **M**u**G** = Matthew 22:37. Visualize a coffee mug with the word 'Union' on it. The mug is on a door mat.

Visualize Jesus standing on the mat as his two legs and feet form the letters <u>L</u> and <u>L</u>. The <u>L</u>'s tells us it's Love the Lord.

... Love the Lord your God ...

Note that the second letter of the three keys words of *Love*, *Lord* and *God* is <u>o</u>. Also, each word is one syllable. Think of Lord as Lord<u>y</u> and the <u>y</u> will lead you into the next word (<u>y</u>our) beginning with that letter.

Jesus replied, Love the Lord your God with all your heart and with all your soul and with all your mind.

Visualize Jesus saying this as he's putting his hand on his *heart* and wiping his *soles* of his shoes on the Mat.

... <u>with all your</u> heart and <u>with all your</u> soul ...

Note the rhythm of the words ... *and with all your* ... with all your heart and with all your soul and with all your mind.

By thinking *soul* as our *soles*, we've covered our body from middle (heart), bottom (sole), to top (mind). That's memorable. Our natural memory will recognize the difference between <u>*sole*</u> and <u>*soul*</u>.

89

In the key word *heart* the last two letters are *r* and *t*. In the alphabet the letter between the *r* and *t* is *s*; *s* for *soul*. The last letter in <u>soul</u> is <u>L</u>. In the alphabet, the letter following <u>L</u> is <u>M</u>; for <u>Mind</u>.

Jesus replied, Love the Lord your God with all your heart and with all your soul and with all your mind.

Jeremiah 29:11 / For I know the plans I have for you, declares the Lord, plans to prosper you and not to harm you, plans to give you hope and a future.

Breaking down the scripture

Bullfrog, u**NP**a**DD**e**D** = Jeremiah 29:11. Visualize a giant frog trying to jump onto his padded lily pad. But, it's no use. It's unpadded.

Imagine four bullfrogs, each with four eyes, assisting Jeremiah onto a four leaf clover. This reminds us that the first two words of the scripture are *For I* (4 eye).

For I know the plans I have for you ...

The four bullfrogs tell Jeremiah, "I have a plan for you to get on this plain four leaf clover."

Four is a familiar pattern to this verse. *For* is the first word. The next word is *I*. Another hint is thinking of four eyes, such as someone who wears glasses. The Lord talks about a PLAN 4 you. *Lord* has 4 letters, *plan* has 4 letters, *know* has 4 letters, *harm* and *hope* have 4 letters.

Also, note that the key word after *harm* is *hope*. These are all 4-letter words beginning with *h*.

... declares the Lord ... The clover resembles a deck. The words *deck* and *declares* have the same sound. The letter *l* in *declares* is a hint that it's the Lord, beginning with L, who declares this.

... plans to prosper you and not to harm you ... *plans* is repeated from the opening verse. *Plans* and *prosper* both begin with the letter *p*. Think of a prospector, who more often than not, fails to find gold because knots are binding his arms, a reminder that it's not harms . The key words in the sentence are: Prospector (prosper), not (not), and arm (harm).

... **plans to give you hope and a future**. The word *plans* is repeated. Writing the words together, *planstogive*, will help to lock it into your memory. Say the words quickly 10 times.

Visualize hopping on your foot. The words *hop* and *foot* are similar to *hope* and *future*.

Read the verse slowly and think about the patterns from the preceding page. As you repeat this verse over, the story of the Prospector will fade, but the true meaning of Jeremiah 29:11 will endure.

Using the words below, fill in the blanks.

Jeremiah 29:11 states ... **For I know the _____ I have for you, _____ the _____, plans to _____ you and not to _____ you, plans to _____ you _____ and a future.**

give   harm   hope   prosper   declares   plans   Lord

Hosea 2:20 / I will betroth you in faithfulness, and you will acknowledge the Lord.

Breaking down the scripture

Fire Hose, o<u>N</u>io<u>NS</u> = Hosea 2:20. Visualize a fireman hosing down onions.

Key words are *betroth*, *faithfulness*, *acknowledge*, *Lord*.

Onions (2:20) are shaped like eyes, reminding us that <u>I</u> (eye) is the first word.

Imagine firemen hosing down onions, shaped like eyes, and bees are flying out of the hose. The bees remind us that the next key word is *betroth*, similar to *bee-troth*. The bees faint; faint is similar to faith.

In pronouncing the word *faith* the letter <u>a</u> is heard, as in …
F<u>aaaaa</u>y-ithfulness.

The letter <u>A</u> reminds us that the next key word is *acknowledge*. To remember that we acknowledge the Lord, the letter <u>L</u> in acknow<u>l</u>edge is the clue we need.

Isaiah 40:31 / but those who hope in the Lord will renew their strength. They will soar on wings like eagles; they will run and not grow weary, they will walk and not be faint.

Breaking down the scripture

Eyes, RaiS**e M**y hea**D** = Isaiah 40:31. To avoid intense heat from a butane lighter getting into your eyes, you raise your head.

but those ... The sounds of the letters *b* and *t* are heard when the word *butane* (beau-tane) is spoken. *B* and *t* are the beginning letters of the first two words of the scripture. Also, notice the ho's in the words t**ho**se w**ho** **ho**pe.

... **who hope in the Lord** ... The heat causes you to hop and leap. From the 12 Days of Christmas, 10 Lords a-leaping is a reminder that Lord follows. *Hop* and *hope* are similar.

... **will renew their strength**. *Lord* begins with the lette*r* *L* and the word that follows the word *will* has an *L* sound. Think of the Lord reigning. Reigns is similar to Reign-new (renew). The Lord reigns.

…**will renew their strength**… The letter *r* is the last letter in the word their. In the alphabet, the letter that follows *r* is *s* and then *t*; a reminder that the following word is **st**rength.

... **strength. They will** **soar on** **wings like eagles** ... *Strength* and *soar* begin with the same letter. The second letter in *soar* is the letter *o* which begins the next word (**so**ar **on**). The rest of the sentence easily flows.

... **they will run and not grow** **weary,** **they will** **walk** ... The words, *they will* is repeated. The last letter in *soar* is the *r* which begins the next word in *run*. *Weary* and *wings* begin with the letter *w*. The sentence has a rhythm to it.

... **and not be faint** has a pattern. Three out of the four words have an *n* present. The words *not* and *faint* have the *nt* sound. The fastest way to travel is to soar, then run, then walk.

Using the words below, write the scripture for Isaiah 40:31.

Isaiah 40:31 / but those who __1__ in the Lord will __2__ their __3__ . They will __4__ on wings like __5__ ; they will run and not grow __6__ , they will __7__ and not be __8__ .

hope   walk   faint   weary   renew   soar   eagles   strength

1 Corinthians 13:04 (Note: <u>04</u> is used not to be confused with 1:34) /
Love is patient, love is kind. It does not envy, it does not boast, it is not proud.

Breaking down the scripture

Shiny red apple, <u>D</u>o you <u>MiSS</u> he<u>R</u> = 1 Corinthians 13:4. You're shining an apple on your shirt as you say to your friend, who just lost his one true love, "Do you miss her? If so, don't worry, love is patient, love is kind, you'll find someone else."

Love is patient, love is kind ... As you're speaking to your friend you bring the apple to your *lip* and *lick* it. *L.I.P.* and *L.I.K.* translates to *Love is patient, love is kind.* There's also the repeating of *Love is*, making it easier to memorize.

... It does not envy, it does not boast, ... Note the repeating of the words *it does not.* Visualize getting *IN* the *BOAT. In* is similar to *envy* and *boat* to *boast.*

... it is not proud. You're getting in the boat in the pond. *Pond* and *proud* have the *p d* sound.

Don't let the last line of the scripture trick you. It begins by reading, *it does not*, then there's another *it does not*, then comes, *it is not.* As a reminder, you can think of saying, "I I" to the captain of the boat. In this case, the I I stands for *It Is.*

Ecclesiastes 3:1-8 / There is a time for everything, and a season for every activity under heaven;

a time to be born and a time to die,
a time to plant and a time to uproot,
a time to kill and a time to heal,
a time to tear down and a time to build,
a time to weep and a time to laugh,
a time to mourn and a time to dance,
a time to scatter stones and a time to gather them,
a time to embrace and a time to give up,
a time to keep and a time to throw away,
a time to tear and a time to mend,
a time to be silent and a time to speak,
a time to love and a time to hate,
a time for war and a time for peace.

Breaking down the scripture

Escalator, MuD = Ecclesiastes 3:1-8. Visualize a giant clock, covered with mud, walking down the escalator. The clock represents time, a word that's used repeatedly in this verse.

There is a time for everything, and a season for every activity under heaven ... This verse refers to time. Time begins with the letter T which is the first letter of this verse (There). The last letter of *time* is the letter e which is the first letter for the word *everything*.

Visualize the clock walking down the escalator during the holiday season. *Season* is the next key word. There's a pattern with the words *for everything* and *for every*. The words *every* and *activity* end with *y*. The escalator is moving down *under heaven*.

Good old fashion repetition will helps to remember the opposite for each word. For instance, when you get to *a time to keep*, you'll be able to know that *to throw away* will follow.

... **under heaven; a time to be born** ... Visualize hundreds of new born babies crawling up and down the escalator. All the babies are balancing a huge plant on their heads.

a time to be born and a time to die,
a time to plant and a time to uproot,

Visualize huge plants killing each other. They are equipped with guns and they're shooting. The killing continues until all the plants are torn down. One plant survives and is weeping and mourning. The plant scatters stones over the dead plants.

a time to kill and a time to heal,
a time to tear down and a time to build,
a time to weep and a time to laugh,
a time to mourn and a time to dance,
a time to scatter stones and a time to gather them,

These stones are unique. Each stone is wearing braces. I didn't know stones had teeth, let alone crooked ones. To remove the braces you need a special key (as in key-p; keep). The key, however, has feelings and sheds a tear and then sighs; similar to the word silent. But in the end, all is good in love and war.

a time to embrace and a time to give up,
a time to keep and a time to throw away,
a time to tear and a time to mend,
a time to be silent and a time to speak,
a time to love and a time to hate,
a time for war and a time for peace.

Fill in the missing words. Remember, there is a time for everything. This time, it's time to memorize Ecclesiastes 3:1-8.

a time to be born and a time to _____,
a time to plant and a time to _____,
a time to kill and a time to _____,
a time to tear down and a time to _____,
a time to weep and a time to _____,
a time to mourn and a time to _____,

laugh   **uproot**   **heal**   **die**   **dance**   **build**

----

a time to scatter stones and a time to _____,
a time to embrace and a time to _____,
a time to keep and a time to _____,
a time to tear and a time to _____,
a time to be silent and a time to _____,
a time to love and a time to _____,
a time for war and a time for _____.

hate   **gather them**   **throw away**   **peace**

speak   **mend**   **give up**

James 4:8-10 / Come near to God and he will come near to you. Wash your hands, you sinners, and purify your hearts, you double-minded. Grieve, mourn and wail. Change your laughter to mourning and your joy to gloom. Humble yourselves before the Lord, and he will lift you up.

Breaking down the scripture

Jam, RooF = James 4:8. Visualize jars of jam spread over an entire roof. The homeowners are outside calling to the jam saying, "Come near the edge." *Come near* are the first words to the scripture.

Come near to God and he will come near to you. The second letter of *come* is o and it's also the second letter *God*. Also, the *c* in *come* and the *g* in *God* make a hard *ka* sound. That's a memorable pattern which makes for a balanced sentence; the hard *c* in *come* and the hard *g* in *God* ... *come near to God.* When you come near to God, he will come near to you.

... **Wash your hands, you sinners, and purify your hearts, you double-minded.** After you wipe the jam off the roof you must wash your hands. When do we usually wash our hands? Before we eat dinner. Dinner rhymes with sinner. And, at dinner we drink pure (purify) water.

Hands and *hearts* both start with the letter *h*. Cut a heart down the middle and you have two sides looking alike. You see double. The word *you* is used twice in *you sinners* and *you double-minded.*

... double-minded. Grieve, mourn and wail.

A *mine (minded)* and a *grave (grieve)* are both underground. The words *grieve, mourn* and *wail* are six, five and four letters, respectively. They act like dominos. When dominos fall we grieve, mourn and wail. ... *wail.*

... and wail. Change ...

Visualize putting coins or *change* into the blow hole of a whale (wail).

100

Change your laughter to mourning and your joy to gloom. Humble yourselves before the Lord, and he will lift you up.

Imagine as you put <u>change</u> in the machine you <u>laugh</u> in the <u>morning</u> as you buy your Almond <u>Joy</u>. No <u>gloom</u> there.

... to gloom. Humble ...

In the alphabet, the letter after <u>G</u> (gloom) is <u>H</u> (Humble). Notice the patterns of the letter <u>L</u>. The <u>L</u> in Humb<u>l</u>e; <u>L</u> in <u>L</u>ord, and <u>L</u> in <u>L</u>ift.

Hebrews 12:14 / Make every effort to live in peace with all men and to be holy; without holiness no one will see the Lord.

Breaking down the scripture

Pot of coffee, we**T** wi**NT**e**R** = Hebrews 12:14. Visualize huge snowflakes falling from the sky. The snow is building until you melt it by pouring gallons of coffee on the pile during this wet winter.

You continue to make coffee and *make every effort to* melt the falling snow.

Living nearby are hippies wearing Peace signs on their tattered and holy shirts. The men assist you with your efforts.

... will see the Lord.

A holy T shirt is a SEE through shirt.

Make every effort to live in peace with all men and to be <u>holy</u>; without <u>holiness</u> no one <u>will</u> see the <u>Lord</u>.

Note the pattern with the string of *L*'s with ho<u>l</u>y, ho<u>l</u>iness, wi<u>ll</u>, and <u>L</u>ord.

... <u>holiness</u> <u>no one</u> ...

There's also the pattern with *N*'s with holi<u>n</u>ess and <u>n</u>o o<u>n</u>e.

Proverbs 10:9 / The man of integrity walks securely, but he who takes crooked paths will be found out.

Breaking down the scripture

Provolone cheese, <u>D</u>ay <u>SP</u>a = Proverbs 10:9. Imagine a day spa where the MAIN (man) INGREDIENT (integrity) is cheese. The massage therapist uses the cheese to rub into your sore muscles.

... walks securely, but ...

The cheese is walking down your back securely to your butt.

... but he who takes crooked paths will be found out.

Then, the provolone cheese takes a crooked path to the fountain. The words *fountain* and *found* have the *fn* sound.

The man of integrity <u>walks</u> securely, but he who <u>takes</u> crooked <u>paths</u> will be found out.

Note the plural words ... *walks, takes* and *paths*.

Isaiah 9:6 / For to us a child is born, to us a son is given, and the government will be on his shoulders. And he will be called Wonderful Counselor, Mighty God, Everlasting Father, Prince of Peace.

Breaking down the scripture

Eye, PaTCH = Isaiah 9:6. Visualize a child born with an eye patch. Also, an eye patch blocks out the 'sun'; a reminder that the key word is 'son'.

... a son is given, and the government will be on his shoulders.

A child is also a son. The key words of *given* and *Government* both begin with the letter *G*.

... will be called Wonderful Counselor ...

The words *will* and *Wonderful* both begin with the letter *W*. When a *W* is turned upside down it becomes the Letter *M*; a reminder that it's Mighty God.

... Wonderful Counselor, Mighty God, Everlasting Father, Prince of Peace.

When the word *Mighty* is uttered it is pronounced *Mighteeee*. The *E* sounds tells us the next word begins with *E*; Everlasting.

In the alphabet, the letter that follows *E* is *F*; reminding us the next word is *Father*.

A Father is also known as Pop. *P O P* translates to *Prince of Peace*.

NOTE: The phonetic directory has 9:6 coded to *beach*, but in this case, *patch* is so much better.

Revelation 3:20 / Here I am! I stand at the door and knock. If anyone hears my voice and opens the door, I will come in and eat with that person, and they with me.

Breaking down the scripture

Revolving door, woMeN'S = Revelation 3:20. See the women's anxiety as she knocks on the revolving door. Here her voice. She's hungry.

NOTE: The phonetic directory has 3:20 coded to *mayonnaise*, but sometimes there's a better word staring right back at you. Such is the case for Revelation 3:20.

John 14:06 / (Note: <u>06</u> is used not to be confused that it may be 1:46) / **Jesus answered, "I am the way and the truth and the life. No one comes to the Father except through me.**

Breaking down the scripture

Toilet Paper, DReSSaGe = John 14:06. The equestrian dressage rider is laying down toilet paper to show his horse the <u>way to lead</u>.

The acronym of Way To Lead (WTL) stands for Way, Truth, Life.

NOTE: Confusion is avoided that we're not in the Book of Nahum; represented by a horse, because the outlandish visual in this scene is the toilet paper. Toilet paper overrules indicating we're in the Book of John.

Ephesians 2:8 / For it is by grace you have been saved, through faith – and this is not from yourselves, it is a gift of God -

———————————

Breaking down the scripture

Fish, KNiFe = Ephesians 2:8. Imagine cutting a fish with a knife in the forest. *Forest* sounds like *For it*; the beginning words in the scripture.

...is by grace you have been saved ...

Once opened, the fish is full of *grease*; similar to *grace*. The grease is saved.

... have been saved, <u>through faith</u> – and this is not from yourselves, it is a <u>gift of God</u> -

You cut the fish through its fat; *fat* is similar to *faith*. In the alphabet, the letter that follows *F* is *G*; for *gift* and *God*.

For it is by grace you have been saved, through faith – and this is not from yourselves, it is a gift of God -

Romans 8:28 / And we know that all things work together for good to them that love God, to them who are called to his purpose.

Breaking down the scripture

Soldier, FuNNy wiFe = Romans 8:28. Imagine a soldier who is also a funny wife. In her <u>hand</u> is a <u>weed</u> and she's tying it up in a <u>knot</u>.

And we know ...

The key words are *And*, *we*, *know*. The *hand*, *weed*, and *knot* are similar to *And*, *we*, and *know*. This helps us to remember the beginning scripture.

After tying it up in a knot, she puts it into her *hat* (that) and throws it down the *hall* (all) landing on *ringworms* (things - work), with each worm having a long *tooth* (together). The tooth scrapes the *floor* (for) onto *goo* (good).

We've now strung together the first 10 words to the scripture;

(hand) **And** (weed) **we** (knot) **know** (hat) **that** (hall) **all** (ringworms) **things work** (tooth) **together** (floor) **for** (goo) **good**

Once we get this running start, our natural memory takes over. The remaining key words are *love*, *God*, *called*, *purpose*.

...good to them that <u>love God</u>, to them who are <u>called</u> to his <u>purpose</u>.

Imagine that <u>God called</u> and we reach into our <u>purses</u> to retrieve the message. It may not have happened to you, but it's happening to our Roman soldier funny wife (Romans 8:28).

Matthew 11:28 / Come unto me, all ye that labor and are heavy laden, and I will give you rest.

Breaking down the scripture

Mat, Da**T**e o**N** / o**FF** = Matthew 11:28. Is the date on or off? Our date arrives, and then leaves. Constantly, potential dates are walking onto the mat and then off. This image tells us that it's Matthew 11:28.

... lab**or and are** heavy **...**

Finally, one date, wearing a lab coat, takes off the heavy garment and lies down to rest.

Come unto me, all ye that labor and are heavy laden, and I will give you rest.

Psalms 27:1 / **The Lord is my light and my salvation; whom shall I fear? The Lord is the strength of my life; of whom shall I be afraid?**

Breaking down the scripture

Palm, NaKeD = Psalms 27:1. In the palm of your hand is a naked figurine. The figurine is under a bright <u>light</u> and is <u>salivating</u>. The naked figurine is wishing for a fur coat. *Fur* is similar to *fear*.

The Lord is my <u>light</u> and my <u>salvation</u>; whom shall I <u>fear</u>?

After the key word of *salvation*, the next key word also begins with the letter *s*; *strength*.

Hebrews 13:8 / Jesus Christ is the same yesterday, and today, and forever.

Breaking down the scripture

Brewed Coffee, hi**D**e **M**y **S**a**F**e = Hebrews 13:08. Each day Jesus Christ will hide my safe where there is brewed coffee. It's the same as it was yesterday, today, and will be forever.

NOTE: written as 13:08 not to be confused with 1:38.

2 Peter 3:9 / The Lord is not slack concerning his promise, as some men count slackness; but is longsuffering toward us, not willing that any should perish, but that all should come to repentance.

Breaking down the scripture

Peterbilt Truck, MaP = 2 Peter 3:9. The trucker pulls out a map, but he's catching a lot of slack from his buddies. He promises that no one will perish as long as they repent.

Key words are *slack*, *promise*, *perish*, and *repentance*.

These words live in the neighborhood of 2 Peter 3:9, part of the VINE system (page 8).

Lamentations 5:22 / Unless you have utterly rejected us, and are very angry with us.

Breaking down the scripture

Lemon, LiNeN = Lamentations 5:22. Imagine tucking the lemon-scented linen <u>under</u>, and then <u>uttering</u> how the linen is <u>rejected</u> by you. The linen is angry.

<u>Unless</u> you have <u>utterly</u> <u>rejected</u> us, and are very <u>angry</u> with us.

Notice all those words beginning with <u>U</u>.

Philippians 4:13 / I can do all things through Christ who strengthens me.

––––––––––––––––––––––––

Breaking down the scripture

Full Lip, ReDeeM = Philippians 4:13. You redeem your full lips to get a new eye, a can, and morning dew through Christ who strengthens you.

(eye) **I** (can) **can (dew) do all things through Christ who strengthens me.**

These 3 visuals (eye, can, dew) get you on the path to remembering this scripture

Note the last two letters of *Christ* (s, t), are the beginning letters to the key word of *strengthens*.

Luke 16:13 / No servant can serve two masters; for either he will hate the one and love the other, or else he will be loyal to the one and despise the other. You cannot serve God and mammon.

Breaking down the scripture

Water (Luke warm), iT** SH**o**T** hi**M** = Luke 16:13.

The first sentence says it all; you cannot serve two masters.

Imagine a servant carrying a glass of water for two masters. One of the masters, named Mr. It, doesn't get his water, so *It shot him* (16:13). Poor servant. He should have brought two glasses.

Acts 1:8 / But you shall receive power when the Holy Spirit has come upon you; and you shall be witnessed to Me in Jerusalem, and in all Judea and Samaria, and to the end of the earth.

Breaking down the scripture

Stage, TV = Acts 1:8. A TV is on stage with a cigarette <u>butt</u>. The TV <u>receives power</u> through one of its <u>holes</u>.

<u>But</u> you shall <u>receive power</u> when the <u>Holy</u> ...

<u>witnessed</u> to Me in Jerusalem, and in all Judea and Samaria, and to the end of the earth.

The TV has a great <u>wit</u> in not only <u>Jerusalem, but in Judea and Samaria, and to the end of the earth.</u>

Note the beginning letter, <u>J</u>, in both *Jerusalem* and *Judea*. Also, in the name Jeru**sa**le**m**, remove the letters L and E and you get SAM; which are the beginning letters in SAMaria.

1 Thessalonians 5:18 / **In everything give thanks; for this is the will of God in Christ Jesus for you.**

Breaking down the scripture

Hairdryer, LouD wiFe = 1 Thessalonians 5:18. At the very busy and noisy salon, a loud wife, with her head under the hairdryer, is shouting "In everything give thanks; for this is the will of God in Christ Jesus for you."

Patrons don't seem to mind.

Psalm 46:1 / God is our refuge and strength, an ever-present help in trouble.

Breaking down the scripture

Palm, hai**R**y **CH**e**ST** = Psalm 46:01. Guarded by a referee for strength, the man puts his hand on his hairy chest.

Key words are, *God*, *refuge*, and *strength*.

Guard sounds like *God*. *Refuge* sounds like *referee*.

In the alphabet, the letter R (refuge) is followed by the letter S (strength).

NOTE: written as 46:01 to avoid confusion for 4:61.

Helpful Hints

* Make note of words that begin with the same letter or have a similar sound and look for words or phrases that repeat.

* Create imaginary to remember.

* Read the scripture slowly and look for patterns. Take your time and don't feel frustrated if you're not getting it at first.

* Close your eyes and concentrate as you repeat the verse. Then check your Bible for review.

* Try to include the first word or words of the verse in your story. This will help you get a running start to remember.

* Get the picture of the chapter and verse, along with the book of the Bible quickly into your story. Each of the 25 examples did that.

* Applying the *VINE* system will avoid any confusion to any scripture you want remembered. Don't hold back. Be very creative. Keep in mind, you needn't tell anyone how you were able to remember.

* If you have trouble forming a picture out of the chapter and verse section, pull out a more visual word nearby. This way, you'll still be able to locate the verse needed because you'll be in the surrounding area to the verse you want to recall.

* To avoid confusion, visualize an empty canning jar for Joshua and a jar of jam for James. Make sure each visual is different.

* Take the necessary time to KNOW the phonetic alphabet. That's half the battle.

* Have fun. Exercising the brain is good for you.

Get yourself into a positive mood when studying the scripture. You've just learned a lot of new information and it may seem overwhelming, but tell yourself you CAN do it. It's a fun way to learn and you'll see an improvement each time you practice.

Opportunities are always there for you to practice. You can quietly go over the verses while you sit in a doctor's office, stand in a bank line, or stride to the mailbox.

Develop your own patterns for remembering. You may want to sing the verses or gesture like a conductor. Find a way which works best for you.

Set up a routine when you study the Bible. Are mornings or evenings better for you? Even if it's for only 15 minutes, set up a specific time and stick with it.

Write down scriptures on 3 x 5 cards. Use them as flash cards and test yourself. Tape the cards on a mirror or in the bathroom. Post the cards on the refrigerator or near the sink.

Organize your thoughts by concentrating on each line of the verse. Think the verse through and let it seep into your subconscious. Take it slowly and you'll soon commit it to memory.

Recite the verse as often as you can. If you get stuck give it a few more minutes before you refer to the Bible. This will force you to concentrate more and will help you to cement the scripture to your mind.

Discuss with others your desire to remember verses. You'll be able to help others and a new Wednesday night study group may develop.

Other books by Paul Mellor include ...

You're Almost There, sights, sounds, and exhilaration from running a marathon in all 50 states

Finding the Keys for Remembering Anything

Memory Skills for Lawyers

You Have the Right to Remember, memory skills for law enforcement

Summer in the Saddle, bike ride across America

STOP Studying So Much, achieve better grades with half the study

Road to the White House, political humor from a politician who knows the angles, yet speaks in circles

Pathway to the Podium, life as a professional speaker

For more information on Paul Mellor's books and seminars, visit ...

www.mellormemory.com
or contact the author at ... paul@mellormemory.com

121